BEYOND WORDS

What Wolves and Dogs Think and Feel

Yellowstone National Park in Winter.

BEYOND WORDS

What Wolves and Dogs Think and Feel

CARL SAFINA

ROARING BROOK PRESS
NEW YORK

To all the creatures; you've been such great teachers.

Published by Roaring Brook Press
Roaring Brook Press is a division of Holtzbrinck Publishing Holdings Limited Partnership
120 Broadway, New York, NY 10271
mackids.com

Library of Congress Control Number: 2019941010
ISBN 9781250144652

Our books may be purchased in bulk for promotional, educational, or business use. Please contact
your local bookseller or the Macmillan Corporate and Premium Sales Department at
(800) 221-7945 ext. 5442 or by email at MacmillanSpecialMarkets@macmillan.com.

First edition, 2020
Book design by Aram Kim
Printed in the United States of America by LSC Communications, Harrisonburg, Virginia

1   3   5   7   9   10   8   6   4   2

CONTENTS

Chula in Winter.

Prologue
Why We're Going

Our dog Jude was sleeping on the rug, dreaming of running, his wrists flicking, when he let out a long, eerily muffled howl. Chula, our other dog, trotted over. This made Jude startle awake. He leaped to his feet, barking loudly, as a person wakes from a night terror with the vivid image and a scream, taking a few moments to get oriented. Then everyone calmed down.

We often say "humans and animals" as though all living things fall into just two categories: (1) us and (2) all of them. But is that the way it really is?

One word we use for the *feeling* behind our desire for closeness—is "love." If an animal such as a dog or cat comes to lie next to you, you assume they love you. I think it's a pretty reasonable conclusion that at least some other animals can feel love.

But let's not just use labels. Let's dig deeper. What makes a *dog*, say, want to lie near you? Why do dogs lick us? What *is* a dog, anyway?

Where did dogs come from? And *why* are dogs friendly and loyal and good at guarding?

We seldom get to see how most animals really live their lives. I've always been interested in how animals live. And so I have studied free-living animals from seabirds to elephants.

When I became particularly interested in dogs, I wanted to know who dogs really are. I wanted to go back and watch their deep ancestors living their wild lives. Well, the ancestors of dogs are wolves. So I started there.

Watching wolves wasn't only a window on our dogs, though. Wolves are one of the most amazing, beautiful, and misunderstood animals on our planet. Watching them really opened a window on who wolves are. And it cast a light on who dogs are.

When my experiences with dogs and other animals—and people—were fewer, I used to think it silly for people to speak of dogs as "family" or other animals as "friends." Now I feel it's silly not to. I'd overestimated the loyalty and staying power of humans and underestimated the intelligence and sensitivity of other animals. I think I understand both better.

Let's go and try to find them. Ready to go?

CHAPTER 1

Wolves at First Sight

From a deep grove of sloping pines, a coyote yips an alarm. And when I scope that slope, my view sweeps across snow, sage, the pines——. Wolves! Nearly a mile away, but clear enough in the telescope, about half a dozen wolves are trotting into the valley like big, long-legged dogs. Like the ancestors of all dogs—which is what wolves are. With an easy, unhurried motion, they cover distance surprisingly fast. Minute by minute, they grow closer. The wolf in front is gray; two black wolves follow closely, one limping slightly; another gray, two more dark ones, and two more grays. Eight wolves, actually. My first ever.

Wolf packs attract ravens, and the wolves of Yellowstone National Park's Lamar Valley attract human attention as nowhere else. The great wolf-watcher Rick McIntyre follows wolves here every day. I don't mean five days a week, or weather permitting; I mean that *every* day—for thirteen years so far, *every* single time the sun has said peekaboo—Rick McIntyre has been out here. No matter the blizzards of winter or the rains of summer; no matter anything else. What matters most to Rick is wolves. Rick has had his eye on wild wolves for more hours than any human ever has. "It's a never-ending story," he says, as if it's that simple. For him, it is.

Rick can glance through a telescope at a wolf a mile away, instantly tell you who it is by name, and recite its life. As Rick sees it, wolves and humans must deal with similar life problems, "such as figuring out when to face the risks of leaving home, finding your place in the world—. There are endless similarities," he says.

Two more wolves who've been lying on the snow on a sunlit slope have just roused. Rick points to two wolves gliding across the snow at an intercepting angle. "The one with the raised tail is Eight-Twenty—that's her."

Some of these wolves wear electronic collars to help researchers track and understand their movements. The wolves often get named for their collar numbers. This one's collar number is 820. So they call her Eight-Twenty. If you have a special receiver—as Rick has—you can sometimes find and identify particular wolves by picking up the collar's beeping signal.

Even compared to two sisters a year older, Eight-Twenty stands out as a particularly talented young wolf. Doug McLaughlin, who manages cabins right outside Yellowstone and comes to look for wolves most mornings, explains: "Eight-Twenty is *so* much like her mother. Even at two years old she's independent-minded, self-confident. She's got the natural-born-leader personality. And she's already an able hunter—which her mother, O-Six, was *famous* for."

The ten wolves are coming together on the valley flats. Deep-chested adults and lanky yearlings. I see them clearly in my scope.

The wolves greet energetically, tails raised and wagging, lots of body pressing and face licking. Rick dictates into his recorder, "Big rally." They're greeting one another the way our dogs greet us when we come home.

What I am seeing is this: Wolves focus on their elders the way dogs focus on their human family. As wolves grow up, they take charge of their own lives and families, a lot like people do. Dogs remain dependent on humans. Dogs are basically wolf pups who never get to grow up to take charge of their own lives and decisions. Wolves take charge. They must.

Rick translates a blur of furry action. "That black one and the gray one on the left are both females and are nearly a year old. The gray is Eight-Twenty's younger sister. She has no collar." Some of the regular watchers have nicknamed her Butterfly. "See her pushing with her paw? That's a puppy thing meaning, 'I want to play.'"

Just to Butterfly's right—two siblings a year older, who helped raise her. Butterfly shows them respect by lowering her body and ears, similar to a human's bowing. "She's very social," Rick says admiringly.

"Everybody's friend." Of course, showing respect helps protect a lower-ranking individual from aggression. Usually.

But now there's aggression and an intense show of submission by one wolf with head low, ears down, and tail tucked. It's the proud and talented Eight-Twenty—abruptly on her back! What's going on?

When their mother, O-Six, was alive, she kept order in the family. But that was a few months ago. Now her daughters are all in competition with one another. Three sisters are now towering over Eight-Twenty. One is a year older, and two are Eight-Twenty's same-age littermates. Eight-Twenty behaves like an older wolf. Her sisters seem jealous.

Pinned on her back, Eight-Twenty is not fighting, just trying to hold her sisters off with outstretched legs. There's a tense pause.

Suddenly, a fierce escalation of violence. The others are vigorously biting Eight-Twenty. This is more than simply putting a wolf in her place. Eight-Twenty is whimpering, yelping, in pain. One sister is biting her in the belly, another on her hip.

When Eight-Twenty gets a chance to move, she runs away. But only a short distance.

She circles back, crouching in intense submission, wanting at least to be allowed to stay in her family. Her sisters aren't open to any compromise; they want her out. Snarling and threatening, they make it clear: coming closer—bad idea.

Eight-Twenty vanishes into snowy sagebrush. This very moment—

banishment by her own sisters—is the final turning point in Eight-Twenty's life.

The main turning point was four months ago, when someone killed their famous mother. The end of O-Six's life started turmoil in the lives of her family.

To understand why O-Six was such a standout individual and why her death so matters, we must go one generation back. Her grandfather was Yellowstone's most famous wolf: Twenty-One.

Eight-Twenty being pushed out of her family by her sisters.

Wolf O-Six.

CHAPTER 2

The Perfect Wolf

"If ever there was a perfect wolf," Rick McIntyre says, "it was Twenty-One. He was like a fictional character. But he was real."

Even from a distance, people could recognize Twenty-One's big-shouldered profile. Twenty-One had the size, strength, and agility to win against overwhelming odds. And he was fearless in defense of his family. On two occasions, Rick saw Twenty-One take on six attacking wolves—and chase them all away!

"Watching him felt like seeing a superhero in action," Rick says. "Like watching Bruce Lee fighting, but in real life. I'd be thinking, 'A wolf can't do what I am watching this wolf do.'" Watching Twenty-One "was like watching Muhammad Ali or Michael Jordan—a one-of a kind talent at the top of his game, talent outside of 'normal.'" And normal for a wolf isn't like average for a human, because *every* wolf is a professional athlete.

Twenty-One never lost a fight. Twenty-One never killed a defeated opponent. Twenty-One was a super-wolf.

*   *   *

Twenty-One came into the world in the first litter of pups born in Yellowstone in nearly seventy years. His parents had both been trapped alive in Canada and brought to Yellowstone specifically to reintroduce wolves into a system that had gotten out of balance. In the 1920s, park rangers killed the last wolves in Yellowstone. They thought they were doing a good thing. But without wolves hunting the elk, there got to be too many elk for the land to bear. In winter, elk suffered hunger. So when the wolves from Canada were released in Yellowstone, they found plenty of food. And they stayed.

But just before Twenty-One was born, someone shot Twenty-One's father.

A wolf does not do well as a single mother. Researchers reluctantly decided to capture her and her pups and feed them for a few months in a one-acre pen.

When humans brought food to the pen, all the other wolves fled to the opposite fence, but one pup would pace a little rise in the enclosure, putting himself between the humans and the rest of his family. This pup would later be given tracking collar number 21.

At age two and a half, Twenty-One left his mother—and an adoptive father—and his birth pack. Twenty-One waltzed into the family known as the Druid Pack less than two days after the Druids' alpha male had illegally been shot. The Druid females welcomed this prime male wolf; their pups loved the big new guy. He adopted the pups and helped feed them. With no hassle at all, Twenty-One had left home and immediately become alpha male of an established pack. It was his great break in life.

Twenty-One was "remarkably gentle" with members of his pack. Immediately after making a kill, he often walked away to lie down and nap, allowing other family members who'd had nothing to do with the hunt to eat their fill.

One of Twenty-One's favorite things was to wrestle with little pups. "And what he really loved to do," Rick adds, "was—to pretend to lose. He just got a *huge* kick out of it." Here was this great big male wolf, and he'd let some little wolf jump on him and bite his fur. "And he'd just fall on his back with his paws in the air," Rick half-mimes. "And the triumphant-looking little one would be standing over him with his tail wagging.

"The ability to pretend," Rick adds, "shows that you understand how your actions are perceived by others. It indicates high intelligence. In those tussles, the pups learned how it feels to conquer something much bigger than themselves. And that's the kind of confidence a wolf needs every day of their hunting lives."

Early in Twenty-One's alpha-ship, three females in his pack gave birth. That was extraordinary. Usually, only the alpha female, or matriarch, breeds. Three litters reflected the unusually abundant food supply. An astounding twenty pups survived, swelling an already large pack to a hard-to-believe thirty-seven wolves, likely the world's all-time largest.

"Only Twenty-One had what it took to run an outfit that large," Rick McIntyre comments.

It wasn't all peaceful. The high density of wolves likely produced more territorial conflict with other wolf families. In territorial defense, or in pursuit of expanded territory, Twenty-One participated in plenty of fights.

Wolf territorial fights resemble human tribal warfare. When packs fight, numbers count, but experience matters an awful lot. As adults of both packs rush to or away from rivals or battle for their lives, juveniles can seem lost in confusion. Juvenile wolves under a year old often seem dismayed by an attack. (It seems even wolves must learn violence.) And a juvenile who gets pinned by attackers may simply give up. Wolves often target the alphas of the rival pack, as if they fully understand that if they can route or kill the experienced leaders, victory will be theirs.

Fatal conflict between tribal groups isn't just a human thing. The second-most common cause of wolf death in the Rockies is getting killed by other wolves. (Getting killed by humans is first.) But as mentioned, Twenty-One distinguished himself in two ways: He never lost a fight, and after he won, he never killed a losing wolf.

Twenty-One's restraint in letting vanquished rivals go free seems incredible. What could it be? Mercy? We might use that word of a person who does not use their full advantage against a threatening opponent.

If a human releases a vanquished opponent, the victor seems even more impressive. Having already asserted dominance by winning, the conqueror who shows mercy displays tremendous confidence. Onlookers might want to follow such a person, one who is so strong yet inclined toward restraint.

History's most esteemed, highest-status leaders are not those ruthless individuals who ruled by force, such as Hitler, Stalin, and Mao, though they controlled hundreds of millions. Peaceful warriors like Gandhi and King and Mandela earn higher global status than violent ones do. The person who has been called the most famous man in the world, Muhammad Ali, practiced ritualized combat in the form of boxing, but he spoke of peace and refused to go to war. Though his refusal cost him millions of dollars and his heavyweight title, his status rose to unprecedented height with his refusal to kill.

For humans and many other animals, status is a huge deal, preoccupying time and costing energy. And for it, much treasure and blood are risked. Wolves do not understand *why* status and dominance are so important to them, any more than humans do. Our brains produce hormones that make us want status and assert dominance. We don't usually even know why. Here's the reason: High status aids survival. Dominance lets you outcompete others for food, mates, and preferred territory—which boosts survival and reproductive success. Like dogs who love car rides simply because they go to exciting places, we don't understand why or how it all works. We just know we want it. One could hardly expect that wolves would understand, any better than we do, what drives us all.

* * *

So back to the question: Can a wolf be merciful? In humans, as we've noted, letting a beaten rival go free is a show of both extra strength and great self-confidence. Releasing a beaten but potentially lethal rival gets you respect.

"Why doesn't Batman just kill the Joker?" Rick asks rhetorically before volunteering his answer. "In admiring the hero who restrains his strength, we are impressed with the hero's power," he says. "A story in which the good person kills the bad guy isn't nearly as interesting as a story where the good guy has a moral dilemma. In the classic 1942 film *Casablanca*, Humphrey Bogart has won the love he has sought. But he arranges things so that the other man does not lose his wife and is not hurt. We admire Bogart's character for that. When we see strength combined with restraint, we want to follow that individual. It greatly enhances their status."

The character in the movie feels bound by his ethics. But do wolves have morals, ethics?

Rick chuckles at the thought. "It would be scientific heresy to say they do. But—"

In Twenty-One's life there was a particular male, a sort of roving Casanova, a continual annoyance. He was strikingly good-looking, had a big personality, was always doing something interesting. "The best single word is 'charisma,'" says Rick. "Female wolves were very attracted to him. People would take one look at him and they absolutely *loved* him."

One day, Twenty-One discovered this Casanova among his daughters. Twenty-One ran in, caught him, and was biting and pinning him to the ground. Various pack members piled in, beating him up. "Casanova was big," Rick says, "but he was a bad fighter. Now he was totally overwhelmed, and the pack was finally killing him.

"Suddenly Twenty-One steps back. Everything stops. The pack members are looking at Twenty-One as if saying, 'Why has Dad stopped?'" The Casanova wolf jumped up and, as always, ran away.

But Casanova kept causing problems for Twenty-One. Well, why *doesn't* Batman just kill the Joker so he doesn't have to deal with him? It makes no sense—until years later.

Fast-forward. After Twenty-One's death, Casanova briefly became leader of the Druid Pack. But he didn't know what to do; he was not a natural leader.

Eventually Casanova, with several young Druid males, met some females, and they all formed the Blacktail Pack. "With them," Rick remembers, "he finally became the model of a responsible alpha male and a great father."

Casanova died in a fight with a rival pack. But every wolf in his own pack remained alive—including grandchildren and great-grandchildren of Twenty-One.

Wolves can't foresee such plot twists any more than people can. But by sparing the Casanova wolf, Twenty-One actually helped ensure himself more surviving descendants.

* * *

Early on, back when Twenty-One was young and still living with his mother and adoptive father, one of their new pups was not acting normal. The other pups were a bit afraid of him and wouldn't play with him. One day, Twenty-One brought back some food for the small pups, and after feeding them, he just stood there, looking around for something. Soon he started wagging his tail. "He'd been looking for the sickly little pup," Rick says, "and finding him, he just went over to hang out with him for a while."

Rick suddenly looks at me, saying simply, "Of all the stories I have about Twenty-One, that's my favorite." Strength impresses us. But what we remember is kindness.

Twenty-One distinguished himself to the very end: He was a black wolf who grayed with the years and became one of the few Yellowstone wolves who died of old age.

One June day when Twenty-One was nine years old, his family lay bedded when an elk came by. They all jumped up to give chase. He jumped up, too, but just stood watching the action and then lay down again. Later, when the pack headed up toward the den site, Twenty-One crossed the valley in the opposite direction, traveling purposefully somewhere, alone.

Some time later, a visitor who'd been way up high in the backcountry reported having seen something very unusual: a dead wolf. Rick got a horse and rode up to investigate.

That last day, it seems, Twenty-One knew his time had come. He used his final energy to go up to the very top of a high mountain. In a favorite family rendezvous site, where he'd been with his pups year after year, amid high summer grass and mountain wildflowers, Twenty-One curled up in the shade of a big tree. And on his own terms, he went to sleep for the last time.

Rick had seen Twenty-One essentially every day of his long life and had watched his career from pup to powerhouse to his final walk across the valley. Before Rick rode up to investigate that day, he had told wolf-watcher Doug McLaughlin that when he got back, he'd tell him what he'd found. Doug saw Rick returning from the meadow, and was anticipating Rick's promised report.

But Rick headed straight to his vehicle. He opened the door, and before he got in, he broke down in sobs. And when Doug McLaughlin was recalling this story for me, he choked up, and I looked down at the ground.

Wolf Twenty-one.

The Lamar wolves.

CHAPTER 3

Packing and Unpacking

A wolf "pack" is just a family. What we call a pack is a breeding pair plus their pups. We often call the breeders the alpha female and the alpha male. Wolf experts, though, consider the word "alpha" outdated. They often refer to the breeding female as the pack's matriarch; she initiates many of the decisions.

The classic idea about pack formation is this: Boy meets girl, they have offspring—pack. Yes, that happens. But with wolves, everything happens. A lot depends on individual personalities and chance encounters. Sometimes two or three brothers form a new pack with two or three sisters from another pack. In a year or two, some of them might split off to form yet another new pack.

Alpha pairs show deep loyalty to one another in matters of defense and assistance. (The loyalty we see in the dogs we love—their "best friend" character—is the wolf in them.) And alphas depend heavily on their children for crucial help in hunting, feeding and guarding pups, holding territory, and defending against attacking rivals.

Extended childcare is a major part of wolf society and family life.

Pups stay with parents for several years. Older children help care for the younger ones. Eventually they leave their parents to start their own families. From dens and rendezvous sites—secluded spots for stashing very young pups—adults take turns hunting, bringing food, and playing with pups, enduring mock ambushes and having their tails yanked by some of the world's most playful, insistent youngsters.

"Wolves are about three things." Doug Smith, Yellowstone's wolf research leader, is counting off on his fingers: "They travel, they kill, and they are social—very *social*. A lot of their life hinges on their socialness—if that's a word." After studying wolves for over thirty years, Doug sums up: "I can tell you this: You can't just say, 'wolves do this,' 'males do this,' 'females do that.' No. Wolves have fantastic individuality.

"If you've seen wolves in captivity," he says, "they're constantly pacing; they just want to *go*." In the wild, wolves travel anywhere from five to forty miles in a day. "Not just to hunt. Also to maintain territory. They're very competitive about protecting their turf.

"A fourth thing about wolves?" Doug is telling more than asking. "They're tough."

During the reintroduction operations at Yellowstone, researchers worried that the wild-caught Canadian wolves might try dashing straight home to Canada. So they kept them for several weeks in large acclimation pens. Most accepted confinement, but three defiant wolves never tolerated it. One jumped high enough to latch onto an overhanging section of ten-foot-high fence, then actually managed to curl his body around the overhanging mesh and escape. And *then* he dug back in from the outside—releasing his comrades. The three defiant wolves' relentless chewing on the chain-link fence caused extreme damage to their canine teeth, basically wearing them flat.

"I thought, 'Wow, these guys are kind of doomed,'" Doug recalls. "But after release, you could not tell there was anything at all wrong. I thought, 'How in the world is this wolf without canines killing elk?'" Wolf jaws exert twelve hundred pounds per square inch, twice that of a large dog. "That's crushing power."

Four or five times, he has caught a wolf to replace a collar and discovered that the animal had a healed-up broken leg. "Since I put their first collar on, I'd been tracking them the whole time; there was *never* an indication that they'd broken a leg!" Once Doug was in a helicopter over a running pack. He was going to shoot one of the wolves with a tranquilizer dart, to make the wolf go to sleep so he could put a tracking collar on. "They were doing the porpoising thing in deep snow. I darted the one at the back. When we reached it on the ground, I was shocked to see that it had only three legs. From the air I couldn't see anything wrong with how that wolf was running." In late winter, another wolf in the same group got a broken shoulder, probably from a kick by an elk or a bison. "She was *ten* years old, and she lasted all the next spring and summer. I think the others were helping her.

"When you examine their bones, you see that these guys have a very rough life *and* they're *incredibly* tough." Doug once saw an alpha female whose leg was dangling; she was attentively watching her pack hunt. Instead of hiding and nursing her break, "she was right there, alert to what was going on." She healed and survived.

He declares, "Wolves never feel sorry for themselves. It's never 'poor me.' They're always—*forward!* Their question is always: 'What's next?'"

Different packs develop distinctive character. The Druids traveled without regard to borders. Mollie's Pack (named after Mollie Beattie, the first woman to head the U.S. Fish and Wildlife Service) established a territory high in elevation, lovely in summer, which in winter turned exceptionally bleak—deep snow and temperatures dropping to minus forty degrees Fahrenheit—and devoid of elk. Only a few big bison lingered—"tough, supersized behemoths," Doug Smith calls them. Over several seasons the Mollie's wolves actually became effective hunters of those thousand-pound winter bison. In one attempt, fourteen wolves repeatedly drove a male bison into deep snow, "a move meant to compromise his footing, his kicking power." Though the bison "literally shook the wolves from his back" repeatedly, the wolves persisted and—after a nine-hour siege—succeeded in killing the bison.

Bison are at the extreme high end of wolf-pack hunting abilities. The bison-killing wolves of Mollie's pack were among the very largest in Yellowstone, with only the hugest wolves able to survive year-round in that cold, going against those giant bison.

*   *   *

Almost all predators hunt prey that's smaller than themselves. Wolves, though, hunt animals much larger than themselves. Their prey is often *five to ten times* a wolf's weight. That takes cooperation. That's why wolves live in groups. Being a wolf is a team effort. That makes wolves highly social. And that makes wolves special.

Predators who hunt animals larger than themselves tend to hunt in organized groups with social structure and division of labor. Only a few are in this elite category, including African painted dogs (sometimes called wild dogs or painted wolves, *Lycaon pictus*), lions, spotted hyenas, and several dolphins, including mammal-hunting types of killer whales. And humans. We're special, too.

Lions move into "wing" and "center" positions, and wingers stampede prey toward centers lying in ambush. Individual lions specialize in playing the center or wing positions, and wing lions specialize in the right or left wing. Bottlenose dolphins sometimes go to work with a division of labor, with some swimming back and forth to block the escape of trapped fish while other dolphins actively catch them. From time to time, blockers move in and eaters take their turn blocking, so the dolphins must have some way of signaling a switch to one another. Sometimes "driver dolphins" specialize in herding fish toward "barrier dolphins." In those groups, individuals tend to maintain these specialized roles.

Humpback whales dive beneath fish schools, then wrap them in a cylinder of rising bubbles called a bubble net, which concentrates panicked fishes. Through these concentrated fish schools, the whales rise and lunge toward the surface with mouths wide open, gulping fish. Humpback whales sometimes form stable bubble-netting crews, with the same individuals seen working together from one year to the next, taking the same positions over time. When researchers watched eight humpbacks make 130 feeding lunges over three days, each whale always stayed in the same position relative to its comrades. As with wolves, these creatures seem to know exactly what is going on, what they're doing and who's doing it, working to tip the odds of survival in their favor.

Wolf hunts might look disorganized at first. Ten wolves might come upon a hundred elk, and what you see, says Rick McIntyre, is that "everybody's chasing different elk. But in the chaos, they're all looking for a sign that one particular elk might be vulnerable. And they all watch each other. It's an efficient way to sort through a lot of potential prey pretty quickly."

Wolves divide the labor. Big males run slower than females and lighter, younger males. (Females range from about 90 to 110 pounds. A big male is about 120 to 130 pounds. The very biggest reach about 150 pounds, not more than that.) In fast chases after singled-out prey, you usually see yearlings and females out front. Younger wolves are frequently the first to catch up to a running elk. They're biting at its hind legs and haunches, slowing it. But young wolves don't know the best way to kill an elk. (And the longer it takes, the more wolves risk fatal stabs from antlers or a kick that breaks a bone or punches out teeth.) Now a big wolf rushes in, plunges past his children and past the elk, and, turning, he lunges up to a throat bite.

Elders often initiate hunts. But younger pack members may not comprehend the strategy. One day Rick watched the Junction Pack's alpha male, Puff, try to get his pack to a higher elevation. Nobody wanted to follow. Rick, though, could see some elk up there. Puff went up high, alone, and disappeared into the trees. And suddenly the elk alarmed and bolted, and Puff was running out of the trees behind the last elk, an adult female. "She was making a lot of bad decisions in her route, and he was gaining on her," Rick says. By now the whole pack realized what was going on. Puff's mate came in diagonally, grabbing the elk's hindquarters. The elk kicked her off, but the slowdown enabled Puff to catch up and grab her by the throat. With a third pack member plowing in, they pulled the elk down. "It's crucially instructive for youngsters to observe how older, experienced wolves manage life and death," Rick informs me.

"Alpha male" is a phrase often used to describe the man who is most aggressively assertive, most dominating—the abusive manager who belittles and yells at everyone, who at every moment demonstrates that he's in total control. A snarling boss is the typical image of the alpha male. Wolves are *not* like that.

Wolves are like this: The alpha male might be a major player in the kill, then go and sleep until everyone is full. "The main characteristic of an alpha-male wolf," Rick says, "is a quiet confidence, quiet self-assurance. You know what you want to do; you know what's best for the pack. You're very comfortable with that. You have a calming effect. Point is, alpha males are surprisingly nonaggressive because they don't need to be aggressive.

"Twenty-One was the classic alpha male," Rick explains. "He was the toughest guy in the neighborhood. But one of his main behavioral characteristics was restraint. Think of a very emotionally secure man, or a great heavyweight champion; whatever he needed to prove is already proven. Think of it *this* way," Rick offers: "Imagine two groups of the same kind—two wolf packs, two human tribes, whatever. Which group is more likely to better survive and reproduce: one whose members are more cooperative, more sharing, less violent with one another, or a group in which members are beating each other up and competing with one another?"

So an alpha male, in Rick's experience, almost never does anything overtly aggressive to the other males, who are usually his sons or adopted sons or maybe a brother. The alpha male just has a certain type of personality the other males recognize. "The only time you'd be likely to see him assert dominance would be during the mating season when the number two guy approaches the breeding female, and the alpha might snarl and bare his teeth, or even just look at him; that would be enough." If the alpha goes aggressively toward the other male, usually by the time he gets to him, the other male is on his back, and the alpha might then give a brief holding bite on the muzzle or neck that communicates rank but isn't intended to cause harm. The other male never resists. He usually just goes down into a submissive posture or slinks away. "You know how a dog sometimes looks guilty when you reprimand it? That's how the wolf looks."

Rick sums it up: "Minimal violence promotes group cooperation. That's what a pack needs. The alphas set the *example*."

Rick describes Doug Smith as a wolf-like alpha male: "Doug is the best supervisor I've worked with, by far. Very easygoing, supportive, very understanding; he never yells at anyone. He has a natural confidence in the best sense. This totally motivates people. People would be willing to work ninety hours a week for him."

I decide to get a second opinion on alphas from the alpha himself. "In the old days," Doug Smith begins, "people talked about the alpha male as the *boss*." Then he adds, "Mainly, male biologists talked that way." In reality, he explains, females do most of the decision-making. They usually decide where to travel, when to rest, what route to take, when to go hunting, and the pack's most important decision: where to dig a den.

Some females seem to be what holds their pack together. Others, less so. "Here's what happened to the Nez Perce Pack: Alpha female gets killed"—Smith snaps his fingers—"pack dissolves. Gone. Leopold Pack: alpha female dies, you couldn't tell; her daughter assumes the breeding role. Seamless."

He tells me, "Personality matters for wolves, a lot." Individual personality determines how playful a wolf is, how they'll hunt, how long a young wolf stays with their parents before leaving to seek their own adult lives, and how they'll lead.

"Couple of examples," offers Smith. "Wolf Seven was the dominant wolf in her pack. But you could watch Seven for days and say, 'I *think* she's in charge.' She *was* in charge. She led by example. So when I use the word 'matriarch,' I mean a wolf whose personality kind of shapes the whole pack."

Seven led by example. Wolf Forty led with an iron fist. Doug emphasizes, slowly, "Very... *different*... personalities." Seven you could watch for weeks; her leadership was so subtle. "You could watch Forty for just one hour and see: in charge and—*mean!*" An exceptionally aggressive wolf, Forty had actually fought her own mother to take her top status. That was *extremely* unusual. (After being deposed by her daughter, the mother wandered out of the park, and someone shot her.)

For three years, Forty ruled the Druid Pack like a tyrant. A pack member who stared a moment too long would find herself slammed to the ground, with Forty's bared teeth poised above her neck. "Throughout her life she was fiercely committed to always having the upper hand, far more so than *any* other wolf we've observed," said Doug.

Forty heaped her worst abuse on her own same-age sister. Because this sister lived under Forty's brutal oppression, she earned the name Cinderella.

One year Cinderella split from the main pack and dug a den. The only reason a wolf digs a den is to give birth. Shortly after she finished the den, her sister arrived and delivered one of her infamous beatings. Cinderella did nothing to fight back, just took it as always. It's not clear whether she gave birth that year. If she did, Forty likely killed the pups; no one ever saw any.

The next year, though, Cinderella, her bullying sister Forty (now age five), and a low-ranking sister all gave birth, in dens dug several miles apart.

New wolf mothers nurse and guard constantly; for food they rely on pack members.

That year, few pack members visited the bad-tempered alpha at her den. Forty's mate—the famous super-wolf Twenty-One—delivered almost all her food. Cinderella, though, found herself well fed by several pack members, including adult sisters.

Six weeks after giving birth, Cinderella and several attending pack members headed out, away from her den. Near Forty's den they stumbled into the queen herself. With "tremendous ferocity," Forty immediately attacked Cinderella. She then turned her fury onto one of her younger sisters who'd been accompanying Cinderella, giving her a beating, too. Soon Forty headed toward Cinderella's den. They were all trotting toward Cinderella's den as dusk settled in.

Only the wolves knew what happened next. But here's what seems to have gone down. This time Cinderella wasn't about to remain passive and let her sister Forty reach her den and her six-week-old pups.

Close to the den, a fight erupted. When a fight breaks out between two wolves, others quickly take sides and join in. In just a one-on-one fight, Cinderella probably would have lost to her sister. But this time there were at least four wolves, and Forty had earned no allies. It was payback time.

At dawn, Forty was down by the road, hiding, barely alive. She was covered in blood, and her wounds—including a neck bite so bad that her spine was visible—indicated an attack of horrific vehemence. One hole in her neck was so deep, Doug said, "I could bury my index finger all the way, with room to spare." Shortly afterward, she died. Her jugular vein had been ruptured; her long-suffering sisters had, in effect, cut her throat.

It was the only time researchers have ever known a pack to kill their own alpha. Forty was an extraordinarily abusive individual. The other sisters decided to act outside the box of wolf norms, to mutiny.

That was remarkable enough. But Cinderella was just getting started. She adopted her dead sister's pups. And she also welcomed her low-ranking sister and *her* pups. And so, that was the summer the Druid Pack raised an unheard-of twenty-one wolf pups together in a single den.

The low-ranking sister, out from under Forty's brutal reign, became the pack's finest hunter. She went on to become the benevolent alpha of the Geode Creek Pack. Goes to show: a wolf, as many a human, may have talents and abilities that wither or flower, depending on which way their luck breaks and whether anyone holds them down or lets them bloom.

"Cinderella was the finest kind of alpha female," Rick says. "Cooperative, returning favors by sharing with the other adult females, inviting her sister to bring her pups together with her own while also raising her brutal sister's pups——. She set a policy of acceptance that allowed the Druids to swell into the largest wolf pack ever recorded." She was, Rick says, "perfect for helping everyone get along really well."

Sometimes a telescope is needed to see the distant wolves.

CHAPTER 4

The Wolf Named Six

In the light of a new morning, fresh powder has turned the ice kingdom into something like a dream. No wind. Utter stillness.

It's pretty, but we've got no wolves in view. So what do we talk about? Wolves.

"She had an unbelievable ability to sense when things weren't right in the pack," says Laurie Lyman, an avid watcher who compiles wolf news for YellowstoneReports.com. She is, of course, talking about the wolf whose birth year became her name, the famous O-Six: most regal granddaughter of the great Twenty-One; alpha founder of this Lamar Pack that we're not seeing at the moment; mentor-mate to Seven Fifty-Five and his big-bodied brother (whose stories we will get to later); mother of the precocious, now-banished Eight-Twenty; and unwitting, unwilling martyr.

"She was the alpha female who most made her own rules in life," chimes in Doug McLaughlin, who never misses an opportunity to praise O-Six. "She did things her way, and did them spectacularly well. The more you watched her, the more you admired her."

"So, big loss. Really sad," reflects Laurie. It's only been a few months, and the pain still shows on faces. Laurie says, "In the park she'd so often seen people. So outside the park, she wasn't particularly worried."

A very unhappy Wolf Eight-Twenty.

O-Six's grandfather was the super-wolf, and O-Six earned her own reputation as both a super-hunter and a master strategist.

One day, Rick McIntyre saw sixteen members of Mollie's Pack— this pack had already killed other wolves—heading toward the Lamars' den. Wolves who discover a rival pack's den sometimes kill all the pups, and any adults in their way. This day, that's just what was unfolding.

On their way, they disappeared into deep timber. All of a sudden seventeen wolves were running out of the trees, away from the den site. O-Six was in front and well ahead at first, but all sixteen enemy wolves were chasing her, and they were closing in fast. She was running across an open slope that meets the top of a long cliff. She was running straight for the cliff.

"I could see that in her panic she'd made a major mistake," Rick remembers. "I knew that when she got there, her only choice would be to turn and fight." But at sixteen against one, that was hopeless. "We'd watched her whole life, and now we were about to watch her death.

"But what she knew—that I didn't know—was that there was a tiny gully that ran across that cliff face, and that it was big enough that she could run it all the way down to the valley floor. So she plunged down along that gully. And when the other wolves got to the top of the cliff, they couldn't figure out how she'd gotten down.

"But a fundamental problem remained: All they had to do was follow her scent trail back and they'd discover the den, where the pups were helpless.

"At that point, one of her adult daughters appeared and did something that I thought was stupid. She just stood, in plain sight. The attacking wolves saw her and charged. She ran east. She was a very fast wolf and, turned out, she easily outdistanced all of them. In the process she pulled them far away from the den and pups." By the end of all that chasing, the Mollies looked confused, tired, and disorganized. They went into the valley, swam across the river, and didn't return.

And those pups that survived that day, because their adults decoyed the attackers, are some of the yearlings we're now waiting for.

O-Six earned a reputation as the best hunter in Yellowstone. People had seen only four instances where a pack of wolves managed to kill two elk in a single hunt. "That was before O-Six got started," Doug McLaughlin is saying with something like pride. On three separate occasions, O-Six killed two elk in the same hunt, by herself.

One day a five-hundred-pound elk and her half-grown youngster emerged from the trees. A hundred yards behind them, walking casually, came O-Six. The elk picked up her pace. Her objective: to get to the river and stand in water deep enough that a wolf would float before it reached them. The elk knew what she needed to do, and accomplished that goal.

O-Six decided she'd take a number and wait. She had once kept an elk in water for three days, and eventually killed it. She lay down on the bank.

The elk split up—mother downstream, young one upstream. As the increasingly vulnerable young one reached a shallower stretch, tension mounted.

"And in seconds," Doug says, "O-Six was suddenly all over the *mother* elk."

While the humans focused on the more vulnerable youngster, O-Six had the situation figured differently: If she attacked the young one, she'd be trying to kill the youngster with a holding bite while the horse-sized mother came on in full fury with sharp hooves flying.

What happened: O-Six couldn't grab the mother elk in the water, so from the bank she taunted the mother into charging. Sure enough, the elk rushed the bank, kicking furiously with her forelegs. O-Six watched for her opening, then leaped up through flailing legs and seized the elk by the throat.

They both tumbled down the bank, falling into the water. O-Six's head was underwater. So she immediately let go of her bite and used her whole body to hold the elk's head underwater. "We saw her demonstrate total knowledge of her prey in a way I've seen no other wolf do," Doug tells me. "And it was the *quickest* killing of an elk that I have ever seen" It can take about ten minutes for wolves to kill an animal by using a neck bite, but "this elk drowned in just a couple of minutes."

Now O-Six had a dead elk in deep water. She tried dragging it out and couldn't. So she planned another strategy. She pulled the elk into *deeper* water, floated it downstream to a bit of beach, and pulled it up there.

She ate some, then lay down to rest on the bank.

The calf, meanwhile, seemed to be doing some thinking of its own. "It had come out of the water and walked clear over by where we were standing," Doug says.

O-Six seemed to expect that the young elk would return to the river at some point. And when it did, it entered not deep water, where it would have had an advantage, but shallow water too deep for an elk to run fast and shallow enough for a wolf to reach. As soon as the young elk did that, O-Six was up and running.

"There was a tremendous amount of chasing, splashing, and thrashing back and forth, back and forth," Doug recalls. "The young elk already weighed about two hundred fifty pounds, and it took O-Six a long time, maybe ten minutes, to get it."

Rick has a story involving O-Six and coyotes. One springtime in this valley, there was a pack of coyotes organized like a wolf pack—pretty unusual—with half a dozen coyotes based around a den site. Coyotes usually fear wolves, and with good reason. But these sharp-witted coyotes had developed a strategy of aggressively harassing single wolves, especially yearlings, who were headed up to the wolf den where O-Six had pups. Any wolf headed toward the pups was always full of food intended for delivery. (Wolves can carry twenty pounds of meat in their stomachs.) The coyotes would surround and threaten the wolf. Coyote extortion. The wolves would avoid severe bites by regurgitating their meat to the coyote bandits, then run away. And the next time the coyotes spotted the wolves, they'd again be full of meat and——. You get the picture.

One can almost hear the coyotes laughing and telling stories. In Native American lore in many tribes including Cheyenne, Blackfoot,

Apache, Zuni, Achumawi, Hopi, Crow, Chinook, and others, coyote is often the trickster. In real life—coyote is often the trickster. One day, four of the coyotes were at the half-eaten carcass of an elk that the wolves had killed, when a single female wolf sauntered in. This is usually the cue for any coyotes to make way for the wolf. Instead, one of the coyotes went to the wolf with a wagging tail as if inviting play—then gave the wolf a sharp bite to indicate, "Four of us, and we're not budging!"

O-Six wasn't laughing. "One day," Rick tells me, she left her den, bringing her whole pack with her, and headed toward the coyote den "as though she'd had enough." When they got within sight of the den, "she seemed to somehow signal her pack to sit and watch. Anyway, they did." O-Six approached the den, and, sure enough, the coyotes started orbiting and harrying her, snarling, teeth bared, heads down, hackles up, closing in.

O-Six ignored them.

She dug into their den. One by one, she pulled out each of their pups. One by one, she shook it dead. And in front of the coyotes, she ate all their pups. "She turned and trotted back toward her waiting family as if to say, 'And *that's* how it's done.' That's the *only* time we've *ever* seen a wolf eat coyotes."

These creatures know what they're doing. At times they let us glimpse their capacity for insight, for planning, for understanding their lives. They know what their own lives are about, at a time when many humans do not. And while I would not trade places, I do admire them. Greatly. They belong.

O-Six, it seems, really did live on her own terms. As a young venturer she'd taken up with a highly competent male who later became alpha in the Silver Pack. But she stayed for only a week or so and then struck out on her own. She'd had many suitors, including some whose status and skill made them worthy of her. She failed to bond with any of them. Rick says, half-joking, "Because she had high standards, she dumped every one of them." He knows that can't be the real explanation, because high standards could never explain her choice of a certain two brothers.

The brothers Seven Fifty-Four and Seven Fifty-Five were only recently independent from their birth pack. When O-Six showed up, Seven Fifty-Four and Seven Fifty-Five took one look at her—and seemed to fall in love. But they had little to offer.

Why she chose so hapless a pair of males as Seven Fifty-Four and Seven Fifty-Five is anyone's guess. Maybe she just really liked being clearly in charge. She was four years old, already a highly experienced hunter who had managed well on her own. They were half her age, and their hunting skills were nowhere near her level. She paid for their undeveloped skills the first year by having to do more than her share of hunting for their pups. And once, after the brothers had fed on an elk she'd killed, their job was to return to the den and regurgitate meat for their pups. When Seven Fifty-Four met O-Six on the trail to the den, he regurgitated the meat to *her*. Doug McLaughlin recalls, "She looked at him like, 'You clueless wolf; you're supposed to do this up *there.'" But later the brothers shaped up.

Wolf O-Six, left. Seven Fifty-Five, right.

And after a while, Seven Fifty-Five earned the nickname the Deerslayer. He learned that though he wasn't as fast as a deer, he had much more stamina. "You can still see that Seven Fifty-Five has the slim physique of a marathon runner," Rick says. "We saw him start chasing a deer way over by Soda Butte Cone; he chased it deep into Lamar Valley. The deer crossed the river and went south again, and he went up along the hill behind the Confluence. Seven Fifty-Five kept pacing the deer, with his eye on it the whole time; and when it finally stopped at one of the gravel bars, he came running downhill and out into the open. The deer saw him coming and—did nothing. Was completely exhausted. Offered no resistance."

"You'd probably guess," Rick continues, "that for every wolf, hunting and killing is the biggest thing on their minds, that they'd like to go hunting every day of their life. But that's not the case." Usually only two or three wolves do most of the pack's killing most of the time. All share. "For some individual wolves, hunting just isn't that big a deal."

For instance, Rick details, Seven Fifty-Four was much bigger than his brother Seven-Fifty-Five, but he just liked to hang out with the pups. He would follow pups around like a shepherd, trudging along no matter where the pups went, and if a pup bedded down away from the rest, he'd go over and keep an eye on it, providing the needed protection. That freed up O-Six and Seven Fifty-Five. They were faster, anyway. But if they were having a hard time bringing down a very big elk, Seven Fifty-Four's size came in handy; he'd just plow in for the tackle and take-down. That's one reason elder wolves matter.

So, that's how O-Six, Seven Fifty-Five, and his brother Seven Fifty-Four became the Lamar Pack. O-Six had been an independent career girl and was four years old the first time she gave birth, pretty old for a wolf to start raising youngsters. She had pups in each of three years.

One of O-Six's daughters from her second litter is the precocious Eight-Twenty, the wolf Rick pointed out on my first morning in Lamar Valley, the one we watched getting run out of the pack by her own sisters.

Rick's and Doug's and Laurie's stories explaining who O-Six was are helping me understand the history behind these particular wolves that I've been seeing, how they came together. I'm about to learn why the pack is now coming apart.

Wolf O-Six, right, being chased by a grizzly bear.

CHAPTER 5

A Shattering of Promises

Cold weather had begun to lock the park down in November, four months before I arrived. It was a tougher-than-average winter in Yellowstone. Most elk and deer migrated directly down to lower elevations, seeking better food outside the park.

O-Six and the other Lamar wolves ventured to their territorial borders. But they no longer found the resistance of other packs. They did find better hunting.

During the second week of November, the Lamar wolves ventured unopposed into lower elevations, traveling as far as fifteen miles or so outside the park's borders. They were in better territory—a lot more elk. It was all new terrain; they had never been there before.

The Lamars could not have known the reason they found no resistance from other wolves at the eastern borders of their usual territory. They could not have known that they had just gone from being protected by a national park and the Endangered Species Act to being targets in a newly opened hunting season. The Lamars hadn't changed. But human promises had.

Because they'd lived in Yellowstone, they were used to seeing people and weren't particularly cautious to remain unseen.

Before there were safe-tucked parks, there was only the world. When Lewis and Clark in 1806 reached the Yellowstone River near what is now Billings, Montana—well outside the present-day park borders— Clark used some of his precious ink to tell us this: "For me to mention or give an estimate of the different species of wild animals on this river particularly Buffalow, Elk, Antelopes and Wolves would be incredit-able. I shall therefore be silent on the subject further."

Yellowstone seems large; actually, it's too small. The park's straight-edge boundaries were created for the tourist appeal of Yellowstone's geysers and hot springs and scenery. How poorly the park would work for wildlife was beside the point in 1872. If animals had to leave the park each winter to find food, who cared? One might as well worry about geese flying south. For deer, elk, and bison, the park is mainly high summer pasture, not year-round range. Winter at seven thousand feet is just too brutal. Come autumn, the whole high interior plateau empties. Of Yellowstone's seven elk populations, six migrate out. Most deer and many bison leave. The area needed by the park's larger ani-mals, the "Greater Yellowstone Ecosystem," is eight times as large as the park. Can a wolf live their life entirely inside the park? It's been done. Could a population of wolves exist entirely within the park into the long-term future? No; it's far too small. Wolves, too, come and go. When they go, many never come back.

In sum, each autumn, as for thousands of years, most of the park's larger creatures drain into lower valleys and skirting plains, looking for the food that might sustain them through winter. But nowadays when they get there, they have walked into a place of bullets.

On November 13, thirteen miles outside the park in Shoshone National Forest, hunters shot a wolf weighing perhaps 130 pounds. He was the pack's largest male. The hunters were interested only in his skin. That skin housed a crucial component of the pack's adult skill and experience. That wolf was Seven Fifty-Four.

The pack retreated to the park, but only briefly. The brothers Seven Fifty-Four and Seven Fifty-Five had been together every day of their lives and had gotten along very well. Fifty-Four's absence was obvious to the whole pack. But because the hunters removed his corpse, surviving Lamars never saw his body. They had no certain way of knowing why he wasn't there. Sometimes wolves simply travel away from their packs for few days, then return. It's hard to say how much the Lamars did or didn't see of the shooting, or could understand about a missing member.

After their brief return inside the park, the Lamars ventured out again. They might have decided to go look for Seven Fifty-Four. Or they might simply have gone for the same reason they were there in the first place: good hunting. Whether they went to grieve, to search for him, to patrol new territory, to hunt where there was more food, or for some combination of those motivations—they went back. They went, interestingly, right near the place where Seven Fifty-Four was last alive.

On December 6, someone killed O-Six.

Her death was a turning point for the surviving members of her family. It was seismic for wolf-watchers, too; they had never experienced such a time as this, when wolves they knew so intimately could get so shot up.

Before people from Europe stepped onto North America, wolves had laid tracks over essentially the whole continent. In fact, for something like three-quarters of a million years, wolves held the entire northern world, from Atlantic Europe east across the continental enormities of the Asian landmass to the Pacific and Indian Oceans, and in North America from the western Arctic to Greenland, south throughout the great eastern forests, west across the Great Plains to the spine of the Rockies, sloping to the West Coast, south into Mexico. That is one exceptionally well-adapted, flexible, and supremely successful social enterprise.

The Endangered Species Act provides the possibility of listing a species as endangered if it faces extinction "in all or a significant portion of its range." Wolves clearly qualify. Wolves have been exterminated from nearly all of their former range south of Canada. By 1930, humans had wiped wolves off 95 percent of their holdings in the lower forty-eight U.S. states and Mexico, where likely over a million wolves had once run. That is why, for decades, they'd been designated endangered.

Their recent reappearances in parts of the U.S. West are limited and few. Federal officials have declared that thirty breeding pairs and three hundred wolves in the entire northern Rocky Mountain region constitute a "recovered" population. For comparison: Three hundred is about one-half of 1 percent (0.5%) of their former numbers there; it's fewer than eight-tenths of one one-thousandth of the 380,000 wolves that once ran the U.S. West. In what is now Yellowstone National Park, fur dealers sold over five hundred wolf skins from 1871 to 1872.

Nonetheless, the federal government has weakened wolf protections. On September 30, 2012, the U.S. Fish and Wildlife Service deleted the words "gray wolf," specifically in Wyoming, from the federal list of endangered species. Open season on wolf killing in the state began instantaneously, on October 1. Every raven knows that the land is one country; the rectangles labeled Yellowstone Park and Wyoming bear false witness to the topography of time and the contours of memory. But Wyoming officials designated their rectangle open to wolf killing year-round. No license required. No limit on the kill. The only good wolf—.

In just over two months, Seven Fifty-Four and O-Six were dead.

———

Wolves are—among other things—group hunters. And many people don't like animals who hunt. Many hunters, especially, don't like animals who hunt.

Wolf O-Six.

After the U.S. Congress established Yellowstone National Park in 1872, poaching was so rampant that in 1886 the U.S. military was sent in to fight it. After hunters on the Great Plains killed tens of millions of bison, the twenty-three bison found standing in Yellowstone were crucial to the salvation of the species.

Predators were treated differently. No protection, not even in the park. After Congress established the National Park Service in 1916, rangers were instructed to exterminate mountain lions, lynx, bobcats, coyotes——. A key park administrator happened to like Yellowstone's bears; that saved them from eradication. Rangers looked for wolf tracks, listened for howls, found dens and pups. In 1926, a park ranger killed the last Yellowstone wolf. There were no wolves across America, where there had once been hundreds of thousands.

For sixty-nine years, no wolf howled in Yellowstone.

You'd think it was elk heaven.

"There is no peace for animals such as elk and deer in a land without predators," Doug Smith is telling me. "There are only alternate sufferings." Either predation—an animal killing other kinds of animals for food—makes them die, or there get to be too many and then starvation makes them die. Predation is dramatic and awful. But starvation causes more widespread suffering for more individuals, a suffering that is more prolonged.

Yellowstone elk populations surged in the wolves' absence. Wildlife managers started killing elk or shipping them to places as far flung as Arizona and Alberta, Canada, where elk had been completely shot out. From about 1930 to 1970, Yellowstone National Park shipped or killed thousands of elk. When that shipping and reintroduction stopped, elk again surged in Yellowstone.

Famished elk and deer so thoroughly scrounged Yellowstone's willows and aspen seedlings that everything from beavers to fish to birds had their lives reordered. No wolves meant too many elk; too many elk meant almost no food for beavers, which meant almost no beaver ponds for—.

As elk fear wolves, one might say that trees and rivers fear elk. In his classic essay "Thinking Like a Mountain," Aldo Leopold observed, "I have lived to see state after state extirpate its wolves. I have watched the face of many a newly wolfless mountain, and seen...every edible bush and seedling browsed...to death. I have seen every edible tree defoliated to the height of a saddlehorn.... Too much safety seems to yield only danger in the long run. Perhaps this is the hidden meaning in the howl of the wolf, long known among mountains, but seldom perceived among men." He offered poetically, "Only the mountain has lived long enough to listen objectively to the howl of a wolf."

———

It's January 12, 1995, right where I'm now standing in Yellowstone Park. A pickup truck pulling a trailer has just stopped. In that trailer: wolves trapped in Alberta, Canada. Six of them—the alpha pair and four male pups—are headed for an acclimation pen a mile south of here. The wolves will be held two months, then released.

After release, that pack decides that Lamar Valley suits them fine. Tens of thousands of people will see them, an experience wolves and people had never shared. A total of thirty-one wolves released in 1995 and 1996 capped a two-decade argument about whether to simply return to this abused block of land its main natural hunter.

With the return of wolves, Yellowstone finished regaining its full roster of native mammals. Mountain lions had snuck back into Yellowstone on their own in the late 1980s.

Wolf numbers flourished because there were so many elk for them to hunt. And because wolves eat elk, the elk overcrowding declined. Wolves helped liberate aspen, cottonwood saplings, and other vegetation from the tyrannical appetites of too many elk. With vegetation recovering, beavers were able to return to streambanks when the wind again whispered in willows. Into the quieted pools behind newly beaver-built dams swam muskrats, frogs and salamanders, fishes, ducks—. Even streambank songbirds reappeared. If the animals and plants in Yellowstone could have voted, a majority would likely have elected wolves. Since their peak in the mid 2000s, wolves have declined, too, as the system rebalanced and other factors also came into play. Of course, the story is more complex, but in broad strokes that's it.

"Yellowstone is the best it's ever been," says Doug Smith, who has worked in Yellowstone since before wolves returned. That's the bottom line.

But a lot of people still fear or hate wolves—and that's the *other* bottom line. Outside of Yellowstone in the U.S. Rocky Mountains, people account for about 80 percent of wolf deaths.

———————

O-Six's collar had shown she'd spent 95 percent of her time inside Yellowstone National Park. Hunters that season shot a total of seven wolves wearing expensive research collars that had been fitted inside the park. Wolf lovers suspected hunters of using receivers to pick up the beeps from the wolves' collars. They weren't paranoid. The website huntwolves.com suggested that hunters, "scan collars; search from 218.000–219.000 Mhz step at .005 Mhz."

"Does it hurt our research? Yes, very much so," Doug told the *New York Times*. "It's a huge blow."

O-Six was Yellowstone's most famous, most watched wolf. The *New York Times* a few days later published what was essentially her obituary, titled "Mourning an Alpha Female." Unlike most human obituaries, hers included testimonials from humans who hated both the deceased and the mourners. One person called wolf lovers "pagans." The president of the Montana Shooting Sports Association likened O-Six to "a psychotic predator stalking Central Park and slitting the throats of unwary visitors." But Nathan Varley of Yellowstone Wolf Tracker Tours in Gardiner, Montana, who earned most of his money guiding wolf-seeking tourists, complained that hunters were killing "million-dollar wolves."

Million-dollar wolves? A study in *Yellowstone Science* concluded that in one year, "approximately 94,000 visitors from outside the region came to the park specifically to see or hear wolves." They spent "a total of $35.5 million in the three states," Montana, Wyoming, and Utah.

The market value of cattle and sheep killed by wolves (the money ranchers would have gotten when they sold them for slaughter by humans) was "about $65,000 per year." Seventy cents from each of the 94,000 extra visitors who spent an average of $375 per person could have easily covered that cost. "Weighing the economic impacts of increased tourism against reductions in livestock production and big game hunting," the study found, "the net impact of wolf recovery is positive and on the order of $34 million in direct expenditures."

So, all of that is why the Lamars' biggest male and their matriarch were shot to death.

The battle rages. Some demand that wolves be protected. Others demand that wolves be killed.

Wolves O-Six, left, and Seven Fifty-Five, right, teasing a grizzly bear.

CHAPTER 6

In a Time of Truce

Native hunters have sometimes had a more sensible, more spiritual, closer-to-truth view of wolves (and other predators, including lions and tigers). Recently, Native American groups such as the Ojibwe have tried to block the opening of wolf hunts. When Wisconsin opened hunting for wolves in 2012, Mike Wiggins, chairman of the Bad River Ojibwe Tribe, responded, "Is nothing sacred anymore?" *Ma'iingan,* Wolf, is sacred to the Ojibwe. "Killing a wolf is like killing a brother," said tribal member Essie Leoso. *Ma'iingan* walked with the first man. (Indeed, wolves orbited dwellings of some of the earliest humans, looking for scraps.) Ojibwe belief teaches that whatever happens to one will happen to the other. In fact, it had; white settlers considered the Ojibwe, like *Ma'iingan,* a competing tribe to be contained. The Western cultural view often sets goals of domination or extermination. The native view of other animals is often long-term accommodation, living with. In sensing deep relationships, Native Americans' belief web is a truth-catcher.

* * *

For a long time, the power in other creatures instilled in humans deep respect and a long, dream-filled time of truce and magic requests in which we asked the stronger, craftier creatures to hold their peace and spare us. As human craftiness increased, respect eroded. Our weapons became stronger. Their strength no longer inspired our respect. We kill wolves and whales and elephants and others not because they are inferior but because we can. Because we can, we tell ourselves they are inferior. As with people's treatment of other peoples, intellectual and moral superiority is beside the point. Usually it comes down to deadly force and what the strong can get away with. The seventeenth-century Dutch philosopher Benedict de Spinoza wrote, "I do not deny that beasts feel," but he said we should act on "our own advantage and use them as we please."

"Might makes right" is an easy, catchy phrase used to justify actions involving everything from meat to men. But might doesn't really make right.

People have come face-to-face with wolves in the backcountry while out alone. Doug Smith sure has. The wolves ran away. North American wolves virtually always flee humans immediately. They don't view people as potential prey. Free-living wolves are known to have killed only two people in North America, one in Saskatchewan in 2005, the other in Alaska in 2010. Essentially, wolves kill fewer people than any other cause of human death. Wolf packs often see and hear vulnerable hikers. And yet they remain shy. One wonders what they are thinking.

CHAPTER 7

Magnificent Outcasts

O-Six's death instantaneously threw the Lamars' alpha male, Seven Fifty-Five, into a very bad position. His brother *and* now his mate and hunting partner were both dead. Even if he found a suitable female to invite into the pack, his now-adult daughters might not allow it. The nine other surviving Lamars included eight daughters and a male pup born that spring. Two of the daughters were almost three years old. They would now be interested in mates for themselves, and higher status. Seven Fifty-Five's problems were many.

With two ranking adults dead and their father wandering the territory trying to pick up the pieces, the daughters encountered two prime males. These brothers had left the Hoodoo Pack, based outside Yellowstone National Park in Sunlight Basin, Wyoming. One was a tall gray in-control wolf; the other, huge, whitish, and mellow-tempered. Breeding season was upon the wolves and they all felt it.

The Hoodoo males found a welcoming reception by the Lamar daughters. But the daughters' gain came at the direct expense of their father, Seven Fifty-Five. With those new Hoodoo males in the pack, Seven Fifty-Five no longer had a place in his own family.

Wolf Seven Fifty-Five.

Hour by hour, colder. Five degrees Fahrenheit. My brand-new boots are rated to sixty below. My feet are not. My feet are cold. I am never really warm. Except when wolves are in view. For the span of any wolf-filled while, I forget that I am, nonetheless, not warm. I've got on snow pants, three shirts, a vest, a parka, earmuffs, my scarf, my fuzzy hat with ear and neck flaps down, and my hood up. We've got no wolves in view.

Temperatures low; spirits high. We get it from the wolves. They don't even seem to notice cold that for us can be fatal.

For a brief while it looked like things would sort themselves out. Seven Fifty-Five lured off a Mollie's Pack female whom he'd previously met. They mated and she became pregnant and he brought her back with him to Lamar Valley. Den sites are special places that exert a strong pull on wolves. Seven Fifty-Five showed her the den that had been in his family's use for fifteen years.

It looked as though Seven Fifty-Five would continue as the valley's alpha male, in his territory. His daughters and their Hoodoo males were outside the park. Everyone had what they needed.

That the Mollie would be the next wolf to give birth in the Lamar den was ironic. Lamars and Mollie's Pack had been enemies. She was probably among the Mollie's wolves who had come to invade the Lamar den when O-Six had given them the slip down the gully at the cliff.

After three months, the Lamar daughters and their Hoodoo males returned to Yellowstone a changed pack. When they detected the new female with their father, they might—or might not—have borne some recollection of her scent from the day the Mollies came to attack. More likely, they simply viewed her as an intruder at their den, or perhaps as competition for the hunting territory. Before dark, the Lamar females attacked and injured her.

But people watching could also see that the black Lamar male pup who was not nearly a year old "wanted to see Dad," as they put it.

"Seven Fifty-Five had been howling behind us," Doug McLaughlin recalls, "and a lot of the pack had answered him, but they were keeping their distances. Yet it was as if that young guy decided, 'I'm a pup; I want to see my Dad,' and so he came up away from the rest and scent-trailed his father for almost two miles."

When he reached Dad and realized a new female was there, "he became confused." He didn't recognize her scent. "He would get on her trail and then backtrack to find his dad's trail. He also wanted to find out who the strange new one was, but he acted like he wasn't sure whether he was walking into some sort of an ambush." So he walked hesitantly, "and when he finally made visual contact, it was like, 'Dad!—but who's *she*?'" The pup crawled over to his father on his belly in intense submission, communicating to both elders that he posed no threat. High-ranking wolves can be a little rough on family members they haven't seen in a while, reasserting dominance. But instead, Seven Fifty-Five wagged his tail.

When the youngster went over to the new Mollie, she'd already been injured by his sisters. She snapped at him to keep his distance. But she also seemed to understand that he had not come to hurt her, that he was young and low-ranking, and that he was known and liked by her trusted new companion.

And that's where things stood when sundown closed the curtain.

* * *

Before dawn, the Mollie female's signal was coming from a different hill. Soon part of the Lamar pack descended from that same hill. Not a good sign.

Seven Fifty-Five showed up on the road in the darkness just before first light. Four of his offspring were by the road visiting with him.

But the two Hoodoo suitors weren't about to tolerate their new father-in-law. Yet the Hoodoos hesitated. They were up the hill across the road, and having grown up outside the park, they didn't like roads. The social goings-on they were watching might have perplexed them. They might not have understood his relationship to their new girls. Or maybe they did, by his scent. Or in the way the others were acting familiar with him, and respectful.

The Hoodoos didn't come down at first. And when they did, Seven Fifty-Five moved off just a little. He seemed unsure about what to do. This was his family. *His valley.* But bottom line, it was two prime males against just him.

Seven Fifty-Five didn't move off any farther. His family stayed put. The Hoodoos didn't advance.

"So then," Doug McLaughlin says, "Seven Fifty-Five crosses the road, to *their* side. They're just looking at each other."

And then Seven Fifty-five turned and just trotted away.

"If they wanted to get him," says Laurie Lyman, "they would have been on him in a *second*. Seven Fifty-Five isn't a wolf afraid for his life. But he has reason to be cautious—these males are huge."

* * *

Apparently Seven Fifty-Five *was* feeling cautious. He continued westward as a lone wolf who never slowed, never circled back to look for his new mate. He'd probably understood by dawn that she was dead.

It's unlikely that a wolf doesn't recognize death, because death is a wolf's living. A wolf requires a working knowledge of "alive" and "dead." When you watch a predator, you sense a skilled professional, experienced and knowledgeable.

How does a wolf *feel* when their mate dies? "This has always stuck with me," Doug Smith recalls. The alpha male of a Yellowstone pack near Heart Lake was quite old. He'd aged from black to bluish-gray, "so we called him Old Blue." Old Blue had reached the almost supernaturally ancient age of 11.9 years (eight years is considered quite old). He'd been spotted struggling to keep up with his pack, and then one day, Old Blue died. The next day, his mate, Fourteen, did something no wolf scientist had ever seen. She left. She left her territory, left the children who were her pack—left her nine-month-old *pups*. Unheard of. "She wandered westward through the snow, crossing terrain so inhospitable it contained not a single track of another animal." Miles and miles later, she paused alone on a windblown slope of the Pitchstone Plateau. Then—she simply continued westward for another fifteen miles. A week later she returned, reuniting with her family. "Though none of us wanted to say she was mourning," says Doug, "I wonder."

Rick McIntyre tells of an alpha female getting killed by another pack. For days afterward her mate howled and howled. So, one loses her mate and goes on a trek alone; one loses his mate and howls— for *days*.

Missing a loved one is why we grieve when a person or special pet dies. Other animals, too, clearly miss a close companion who's died. While they are alive, they call to one another, look for one another, and return to the same nest or den. Their behavior clearly shows that they envision their mates and their dens and homesites. They anticipate their mate's return. When the mate vanishes, the survivor continues to look for them. They know who they are looking for. In other words, they miss them. Then, as with us, they adjust and life goes on. Sometimes it goes on in a very changed way.

Seven Fifty-Five didn't stop putting distance between himself and his estranged family until he was well past Hellroaring, approaching the Blacktail Plateau, something like twenty miles as the raven flies. In all his life, he'd never before been there.

Just weeks earlier he'd been the proud alpha male of the whole Lamar Valley, mated to Yellowstone's best hunter and backed by his enormous, gentle brother and three generations of offspring. Imagine his situation. He has in the last four months lost his brother and mate to humans, and because of that he lost a *new* mate to his own daughters. His daughters have attracted hostile males he cannot handle; he is no longer safe in his own home among his own family. At the bitter end of winter, he has no help hunting, and no hunting territory. Going into pupping season, he has no mate. Basically, his life is over.

And we've seen the jealous sisters collude to eject their precocious sister Eight-Twenty.

"Hunters like to say that if you take out an alpha, it doesn't matter," says Laurie Lyman, the former schoolteacher. "It matters. The pack becomes a classroom with no teacher."

Ironically, the Lamars' two most competent survivors are now the outcasts. The alpha male *Seven Fifty-Five* and his talented daughter Eight-Twenty are now the ones most radically affected, each out alone, their prospects sketchy at best.

I had known that a wolf pack is a family, a breeding pair plus their offspring, who help raise the youngsters. I had known that as offspring matured, they left to make their own lives, start their own packs. What I had not imagined was the politics involved, the personalities, the paybacks and coalitions, the family turmoil following tragedy, the loyalties and disloyalties. It seems all too human.

———— ❦ ————

A light all-night snow has re-wintered the slopes and valleys. First light colors the fresh powder pink. Sixteen degrees Fahrenheit.

Thousands of miles east, back home on my sea-level coast, spring peeper frogs are calling from vernal wetlands and returning ospreys are reclaiming their immense nests. But here at seven thousand feet, winter holds a grudge. The only meager sign of spring is a half dozen geese motoring overhead. Yet the fresh snow is just a lie; the down-jacketed geese know that the sun's longer days tell the truer story.

After lots of searching, we find wolves on a high slope, bedded down. The Hoodoo males are looking very much at home among the Lamar wolves. Tall Gray is sleeping at the edge of a snowdrift with his chin on the new powder, his paws hanging over the ridge. He is acting alpha. When the yearling male pays his respects, both new Hoodoos greet him, friendly, licking faces and wagging tails. This pack is settling down, relationships nearly sorted out.

A radio crackles. Two wolves have appeared a couple of miles up-valley, and their beeps confirm identities: Seven Fifty-Five and his banished daughter Eight-Twenty are together. We go.

High on a ridge above an open snowy slope, near the end of vision even in our telescopes—there they are, traveling. Seven Fifty-Five already has covered an astounding amount of ground since yesterday. All the way to Hellroaring and back, maybe forty miles round-trip. He knows this valley as his home, and he knows Eight-Twenty as his daughter. So in this immensity of miles and snowy mountains and timber and sage, they've found each other.

At about six miles per hour, they're covering significant landscape. Eight-Twenty is trotting along, holding her tail straight out behind her—an alpha posture. She's feeling good. At age two, she is a prime-of-life young-adult wolf, classic gray coat pattern with darker grizzled cape, light cheeks. He is a born-black wolf silvered toward seniorhood, with a fifth birthday coming up in two weeks. He has already outlasted most Yellowstone wolves, whose lifetime average is intensely short, just under three and a half years. They are running now, across snowy slopes in and out of timber.

How very wolflike of them to have found each other. How very human of us to share their relief at being together. But I predict the happy time will be short. A new beginning isn't so simple.

With Eight-Twenty's alpha personality, she'd likely not stick around if her father acquired a new mate. Likewise, if Eight-Twenty herself got a new mate, the situation would be intolerable for her father. And there is the detail of territory; where could they hunt? Eight-Twenty and *Seven Fifty-Five* are now, in fact, only about a mile, line of sight, from the rest of their family—the wolves who have given them such trouble.

Meanwhile, the main Lamar group is back to slumbering. We hang around in the cold watching wolves sleep. One yearling wakes, trots to a hidden spot, reappears with part of an elk's lower leg, and lies down, happily chewing like a pooch with a bone.

Around three in the afternoon, the Lamars rouse and rally. Then the pack begins howling. The humans fall silent.

Their voices surprise me, higher than the deep, chesty bawls I'd expected. And unexpectedly varied: some yowling and others yipping, some wavering their tones, others singing long, spare notes that they hold and let taper, the singing so different among the vocalists. And the impression—when I close my eyes—is of many more voices than there are wolves.

The howling fills the valley, seeming to my human brain solemn and yearning as a sacred chant in a cathedral. It reaches right into me. I hear affirmation and mournfulness. But how do *they* mean it, and what do *they* hear? Rallying cry? Emotional release? A warning? Whatever they are saying and however wolves hear it, the impression on me is of some ancient story, wordless as a dream at dawn.

If Eight-Twenty and Seven Fifty-Five howl back, it could provoke a violent confrontation among wolves who now all hold a deep claim to this valley. All players understand the dynamic. Eight-Twenty and Seven Fifty-Five shrewdly maintain silence.

But they can't hide in this valley any more than they can avoid leaving scent as they travel through. Sooner or eventually, push will come. Wolves and people want their once-and-for-alls. Eight-Twenty and Seven Fifty-Five are in a bind.

She melts into deep timber. He follows. The howling trails off until the air is again filled only with sunlight and cold.

Hours later at around 6 P.M., Eight-Twenty starts howling.

Tactical mistake. Immediately the Lamars rouse, answer—then mobilize.

The Hoodoo brothers have no quarrel with Eight-Twenty. But with the females leading, the Lamars are heading directly to where they've heard their banished sister's wails.

They vanish into some low timber and reappear high on a flat stretch of land above a snowy swath on a wide mountainside.

Eight-Twenty appears at a long distance away. Eight-Twenty's late-day calling was likely intended to locate her dad, Seven Fifty-Five. But he has vanished utterly. No beeps. She has failed to draw her only remaining friend in the world. She has drawn all her new enemies.

Eight-Twenty is a superior wolf among average sisters of similar ambitions but lesser abilities. Wolf politics are tricky. Even a wolf can be too good for her own good, and made to pay. We're seeing it playing out in the politics of this pack, before our eyes.

Light fades with Eight-Twenty traveling but with tail tucked this time. She's looking unhappy and dispirited. I can see the pack and I can see her. I can't tell if they have one another in sight, but clearly they all know who's where.

Wolves O-Six on right, and Seven Fifty-Five.

Ravens gather round to feast.

CHAPTER 8

Where the Wolf Birds
Lead Us

Eight-Twenty and her father spent less than one day together. Now Seven Fifty-Five's collar signal cannot be located by handheld antennas waved in winter air. He has left this valley. Eight-Twenty, companionless but detectable, stays out of view.

The deaths of Seven Fifty-four and O-Six completely unraveled the calculus of life in the politics of the pack. Death takes not just the lives of wolves killed; it changes the prospects of survivors, even descendants. Individuals matter. A wolf is not an "it." A wolf is a "who."

Laurie searches the valley as a raven might, carefully scrutinizing all details for signs of tracks, a bit of movement, the ground beneath an eagle in a tree—anything.

I see—nothing.

When Laurie says, "I have them," she might as well have pulled rabbits out of her hat. My question: Where? I am looking where she's looking. I still see—nothing.

She steps aside with an inviting gesture, and when I put my eye to her telescope I see—and this is incredible—eight wolves at a kill *two miles away.* Looking in that direction with my binoculars, I see an oblong dark smudge. Black pepper on snow. The ravens. Of course.

By the time wolves kill an animal they've been chasing, ravens are already arriving. This has been going on so long that ravens have been called wolf birds. Wolf kills often attract ravens by the dozen.

In Norse mythology, the god Odin, though father of all gods, had certain shortcomings of sight and memory and knowledge. Odin drank only wine and spoke only in poetry. He needed help getting by. Compensating for his godly shortfalls were the two ravens Hugin and Munin—mind and memory—who perched on his shoulders to bring news of the wide world, and two wolves at his side, who provided meat and nourishment. All were one god-man-raven-wolf superpack. The power resided in the combination within that coalition. Biologist and author Bernd Heinrich wondered aloud whether the Odin myth captured "a powerful hunting alliance, a past we have long forgotten as we abandoned our hunting cultures to become herders and agriculturists." And ranchers.

Wolves, apes, elephants, dolphins—obviously smart. But birds have a lot going on despite having much smaller brains. Especially wolf birds and their crow family relatives, the jays, magpies, jackdaws, rooks—. They're *smart.* They're keenly observant, and some share with dolphins, elephants, and some carnivores a tool kit of reasoning, planning, flexibility, insight, and imagination—at an ape's level of intelligence.

In Yellowstone, where ravens have dotted their black exclamation points onto the white pages of the snows of many thousands of winters, they've taught themselves something new: how to unzip hikers' packs. The relative size of the forebrain—the "thinking" part—in ravens and their relatives is significantly larger than in other birds, with the exception of some parrots. A raven's brain is the same size relative to its body weight as a chimpanzee's. Some scientists credit this forebrain enlargement as the thing that gives members of the crow family "primate-like intelligence."

In a test, ravens encountered something they'd never seen before: meat hanging on a string. The only way to get the food was to pull the string up a little with the bill, clamp a foot on the string after each pull, and repeat till the food was in reach. Some ravens nailed this solution on their first encounter. Just by looking at it, they understood cause and effect and could *imagine* the solution. They didn't fumble around with trial and error. In other experiments a raven could rapidly solve a puzzle that left a human toddler and two poodles acting like they "don't even realize there's a puzzle to solve."

Now let's get personal. Betty is a New Caledonian crow who uses previous experience to reason through problems. Having learned what a hook is, she bends straight wire into hooks to reach food deep inside tubes. Presented with an array of wires, Betty chooses the correct length and diameter for the task before her. There's no reason to suspect that Betty is exceptional among New Caledonian crows. She just happened to find her way into an experimental situation with a bunch of humans. New Caledonian crows can use tools to solve an eight-step puzzle to get at food. (You can watch it online.)

In an experiment, crow-like rooks had no difficulty figuring out a clear plastic apparatus that required the birds to drop a stone down a tube to release a tasty grub. Plus—they chose the largest of several available stones. When experimenters narrowed the tube, three out of four birds immediately chose *smaller* stones that would fit the narrower tube; they didn't even try the larger stones they'd previously used. When they could not get a stone but were given a stick, all the tested rooks immediately inserted the stick into the tube, then pushed down to release the treat. When experimenters gave them a stone that was too large plus a stick that would work *or* a stone that would work plus a stick that was too short, each bird—on the first try—chose the tool that would work. When given a stick with side branches that needed to be snapped off before it would fit down the tube, each rook handily snapped the branches off. When the grub was in a little bucket in a tube and the rooks were given a straight piece of wire, they all made a hook to snag the bucket handle and get the snack. They knew what they wanted, and they understood what they were doing to get it. This is true insight. Cockatoos, which are parrots, also use insight in solving never-before-encountered puzzles involving locks, screws, and latches.

Crows remember—for years—the faces of researchers who have

caught and handled them for purposes like marking and measuring. When they see those people walk across a university campus, they loudly scold them. From those scolding crows, other crows learn who these seemingly bad and dangerous individuals are, and give warning alarms at the sight of them. Some researchers started wearing masks or costumes when catching crows so that they wouldn't be yelled at for years afterward.

These birds and we apes have differently structured brains. (We have the mammal neocortex with ape enlargement, and they have the bird nidopallium with corvid enlargement.) But as they say, great minds think alike. We have converged on some of the same mental abilities. Researchers wrote, "New Caledonian crows and now rooks have been shown to rival, and in some cases outperform, chimpanzees in physical tasks, leading us to question our understanding of the evolution of intelligence." Scientists concluded that, overall, ravens, crows, and their kin "display similar intelligent behavior as the great apes." Who knew? And what else don't we understand?

Wolf O-Six.

CHAPTER 9

Wolf Music

We hop in our vehicles and convoy east. From directly across the valley, it's now easy to see black ravens on white snow surrounding a reddened patch. Into focus in my scope come several rouge-faced Lamar wolves yanking mightily at the newly exposed rib cage of a freshly killed elk they're rapidly reducing to a bony rack. The elk's severed head, with its crown of sharp antlers, lies in the snow like a set-aside trophy. Little seems left for the ravens and magpies, but their presence and patience assure them it will be enough. Working such kills is their profession. In all, nine wolves attend. Seven, bellies already full, sprawl contentedly on nearby snowy ground.

Think about what's happening: An elk who ran for its life is being converted to wolf flesh and wolf bone and wolf nerve that chases elk who run for their lives to avoid the fate that is pursuing them, a fate built entirely from creatures just like themselves. Overhead the sky livens with playful croaks of ravens who are also largely made of elk. Later, the predator's life will end, its body become grass. Grass again becomes elk, and on it goes.

I stamp my feet to see whether they're still there. As we stand around waiting for the wolves to sleep off their food coma, we watchers watch, chat, snack, compare boots and gloves again, and generally do everything except warm up. Rick McIntyre starts telling me about a sickly yearling named for the white triangle on his chest. It was bad times. The pack was rife with mange that was sapping their strength, and rival wolves had killed their matriarch.

One morning, Triangle the yearling and his three-and-a-half-year-old sister were confronted by three hostile wolves. Triangle and his sister ran and—perhaps as a strategy or just in sudden panic—split up. The intruders pursued the sister. She was the pack's fastest runner, but one of the attackers caught her and pulled her down. She instantly jumped up, wheeled, and ran for the river. He caught her twice more; she jumped up each time, running with all she had.

When tackled for the fourth time, all three brothers piled in. Now she was on her back fighting desperately, with two wolves violently shaking their heads as they were biting her belly and hindquarters while the biggest wolf moved in and clamped his jaws on her throat for the killing bite.

As she continued fighting, the big wolf, confused that his bite had not killed her, stepped back. He had bitten into her radio collar housing. But he seemed to figure it out and repositioned for a bite that would avoid the collar. Rick was watching through his telescope, and in that instant a small black blur turned the scene to chaos. It was

Triangle, the sick little yearling, in effect trying to snatch his big sister from the jaws of death.

Two of the attackers chased him. His sister leaped to her feet, streaking toward the river. Triangle only briefly distracted all three attackers. They caught his sister just as she reached the riverbank, and all four tumbled into the water. She had no chance against them all. But Triangle again rocketed in. In the confusion, his sister splashed across the river and, emerging with a seriously bleeding gash in her chest, ran across the valley and upslope to the north, toward her family's den.

Meanwhile, the three males were all chasing Triangle. And in a race that might have set a record in beating the odds, the small, sick wolf outran his tormentors. They gave up and went off across the valley at a slow trot, headed south.

A week and a half passed before Triangle's big sister reappeared. She survived her wounds and got well. Triangle continued to hunt and be seen with the pack for months, but over time his mange infection and his injuries from the fight must have weakened and eventually overcome him.

Rick considers Triangle "a hero."

Hmm. Humans can be heroes, but can wolves? What could Triangle have been thinking?

Rick says, "We judge heroism not by what is thought but what is done." If a hero is someone who risks their life for the life of another, then what about Triangle the sickly little-brother wolf who saved his big sister? Well, you tell me.

*   *   *

After a couple hours of snoozing, the Lamars wake and rouse, enjoy an enthusiastic greeting rally, and then fan out just a few paces and begin howling. The human chatter quickly dwindles to silence as we listen. The deep fascination. Felt. Yet inexplicable. The wolves' voices waver, change pitch. Both gleeful and mournful. Haunting.

We pay rapt attention to their singing. It's seems to matter to us somehow.

Sound sometimes carries emotion across species. Dogs understand when people are arguing. And we understand a growl as a warning. Some of the emotional freight carried by animal sounds has ancient roots. Our shared capacity to perceive it is part of our deep inheritance. Whether the receiving ears belong to a human infant, a dog, or a horse, several short upward calls cause increased excitement, long descending calls are calming, and a single short abrupt sound can pause a misbehaving dog or a child with a hand in the cookie jar.

You know whether people are arguing even in a language you can't understand because of their tone of voice. The word for the meaning that is carried by tone is "prosody." Singing in another language presents some of the purest prosody; we don't understand the words, and we respond entirely to vocal sounds and rhythmic patterns. Hearing music changes our brain chemistry, leading to, for instance, increased levels of the hormone norepinephrine and the sense of well-being it produces.

Music by humans is designed for humans' range of hearing and preferred tempo. Most other animals don't respond much to human music. Some do. Our green-cheeked conure, Rosebud, struts a lively dance to music that has a strong beat, especially if we bring out the percussion toys. There are plenty of online videos of dancing parrots, such as Snowball the sulfur-crested cockatoo.

Sound can convey emotional *qualities* such as anger, fear, joy, affection, sadness, and excitement, plus varying *intensities* of those emotions. Music can capture and convey these emotions. Researchers have noted that "music is one of the best forms of emotional communication known." The emotion in music affects your own emotions; exciting music gets you excited. Feel the music.

After the haunting howling vanished into the thin air, the wolves ate a little more, then enjoyed some romping play. Then another food coma. When two coyotes came to the carcass, the wolves, lying on the snow less than twenty yards from the rack of bones, were so gorged they didn't care. They will eat and sleep all through the following day and night. I leave them to their wolf dreams. Voices come and voices go. The song remains. But songs, too, can be silenced.

———— ◦◦◦ ◦ ————

At dawn, it's minus three degrees Fahrenheit. Another wintry springtime day. Another fairy dusting coats Lamar Valley with a new white-powder quilt. Stillness, silence.

I'm alone, determined in this iron cold to discover wolves on my own. I scope along the valley's far slopes, searching for wolves by not looking for wolves. I'm looking for a pack's tracks somewhere in the fresh snow, maybe ravens gathering—.

Doug McLaughlin arrives.

Intent on finding something good before he does, I am glassing down one particular snowfield when he says, "Got one."

On the far skyline of a snowy bench above timber walks a wolf. A gliding bald eagle leads me down, down the snowy slope. And just at the toe of that slope, where it meets the expanse of the valley floor, I discover a riddling of tracks and a broad patch of hair and blood and ravens. Down now behind a very slight rise, I see just the head of that eagle, pulling energetically on something. So the main carcass is there, barely out of view.

Almost directly upslope—Doug points this out, too—that eagle's mate is already on eggs, sitting on a huge stick nest in a cottonwood canopy. I've never been in a place where spring and winter collide so forcefully. A coyote trots in and begins tugging jerkily on the piece of the carcass that the eagle was working.

Now a total of nine Lamar wolves, four blacks, five grays, just coming out of timber, are descending the long slope, breaking a new trail in the snow, past the patch of scattered hair and blood, strolling toward the carcass as casually as if returning to the salad bar for seconds. The sister on the left is acting every bit the alpha. Her low-ranking litter-mate sister, Middle Gray, is walking next to her. They seem peaceable with each other right now.

The coyotes sense the wolves' supreme assurance. In core territory, well fed, warm in their fur, the wolves are in charge and, essentially, untouchable.

One wolf pulls up into view the red rib cage and spinal column of an elk. No head. Another wolf pulls a big piece of hide. Others pull off individual ribs or find leg bones and plop down, chewing contentedly. These wolves need about three elk per week. Less than a mile away from the belly-full wolves, I see three elk browsing peacefully on the river's willowed banks.

After the wolves have fed, and fed again, the nearly-yearlings chase and play bitey-face, just like our dogs at home. You'd think wolves wouldn't need to play snap-dragon after actual big-game hunting and a massive gorge. But apparently wolves need balance in their lives, too.

After the frolic, they drift a few yards and scatter like furry throw rugs, sprawling as if they were at the beach, making no attempt while lying on the snow to curl up or conserve heat. They are neither cold nor hungry. That's the difference between them and me.

Middle Gray wakes. She's a sweet-tempered, pup-loving three-year-old. Her domineering sister—the same sister who won't tolerate Eight-Twenty—is the source of her low status. Middle Gray disappears uphill.

"Is she looking for Eight-Twenty?" Laurie Lyman wonders aloud.

*   *   *

A couple of hours later, the rest of the pack members wake, stretch, pee. They rally: tails wagging, licking faces. A little bit of bounding play. For several minutes, all howl. Then all rest.

An hour later Rick gets a strong signal from Eight-Twenty. She's in line with the wolves sleeping on that slope. Approaching them? She must be conflicted.

Her hostile sister remains asleep.

A while later, it's clear that Eight-Twenty is some distance away from the rest—and staying there.

"And where's 'Fifty-Five?" Laurie would like to know. Seven Fifty-Five isn't beeping in. All day yesterday he wasn't heard from.

"He has good reason to be afraid," Doug comments. They talk without taking their eyes from their scopes, searching for a glimpse of Eight-Twenty.

Laurie agrees but reminds us, "If those males really wanted to kill him? They would have done it the last time."

Midmorning, snowing heavily. Nobody moving much.

Earlier, somebody had seen a grizzly ambling into the willows at the Confluence. Because we don't have anything better to do than drive in a snowstorm, we travel a couple of miles to there. It's where the braiding channels of Soda Butte Creek join the Lamar River.

In the waters of March, an otter is swimming upstream in a blizzard.

The bear had been at an old elk skeleton that's poking through the snow. Rousing from hibernation into the wintry side of spring, the bear likely spent a nighttime cracking elk marrow bones, perhaps even the frozen skull. Winter carcasses maintain value here for weeks, feeding many. Wolves, coyotes, foxes, ravens, eagles, magpies——. Life depends on death. As Wolf reaps, so Wolf sows.

A black Lamar wolf who had been sleeping where we just came from—is here! What? And now we see that the pack has somehow drifted through the snow ahead of us. We had seemed to leave them to drive here. And here they are. Like magic.

In heavy-slanting snow, they almost float. This is the closest we've been, only about a hundred yards between us. As I am binocular-eyeful of the Hoodoo man Tall Gray trotting along a willow thicket, his amber eyes shoot me a straight glance. But he shows no interest, and his gaze doesn't hold.

After sniffing the frozen bones, they all sprawl in blizzard contentment, as snugly at home on the snow as Chula and Jude on our rugs.

Fog and a heavier horizontal snow squall descend briefly like a whiteout curtain, and when the curtain rises, all the wolves have somehow ghosted from view.

————

At three-thirty in the afternoon, I am no longer in Lamar Valley. Two distant, unseen wolves are howling back and forth across some span of air, of time. The howls grow a little fainter and a little stronger. These wolves are moving. Who are they? Like smoke signals of sound, howls continue rising into the air at intervals. The message is one we can't yet decipher.

We get just a glimpse of a black wolf traveling across a small clearing on a heavily timbered slope. Neck hackles looking feathery, legs lanky, this individual is younger than two years. But that's all we can tell. This wolf is going *away* from the other caller, who seems to be trailing.

Taking my eye from the scope, I watch the moving black grain that is the wolf disappear over a ridge. We drive two miles to get a view of the mountain's opposite slope and stand there, waiting, as the temperature drops, hoping for the black grain to reappear.

Two hours later we're still waiting, now occasionally hearing the same wolves' muffled howls. They're coming.

Four hours since our glimpse. Occasional howls traded. No further glimpses. We can hear that the black one we saw is still traveling and howling.

There is the black wolf again!

And from a hill at least a mile from that black traveler, but now suddenly clear in open air, a strange cry rises. Part howl, part wail. A long, pained, yearning smudge of sound. The word is: anguished. Is that what this caller feels? A lone gray wolf steps onto the skyline on the slope above us, looking down on the valley, looking to where the black one—just a moment ago—appeared and vanished.

The black wolf, continually howling though again unseen, continues moving away from the gray.

I glance back up to the gray, who shows the indecisiveness of a lost dog, turning this way, then that. The gray wolf finally decides to turn *away*, trotting up and over the back of the ridge on which it suddenly appeared, toward where it came from.

"The black one *has* to be Jet Black," Laurie says. A young female of the Junction Pack.

"The gray *has* to be Seven Fifty-Five." That's Doug's opinion.

A long silence seems to settle. And yet—am I still hearing him or are my ears playing tricks? His yearnful howling seems lodged in my head, and I almost think I hear it continually haunting the thin breeze.

My companions shake their heads; they're not hearing what I'm hearing.

Rick calls on the two-way radio. Seven Fifty-Five's signal is coming in. Not far from the Junction Pack. And Eight-Twenty's signal is coming in, too, from Slough, not too far from her father.

Is that why he just turned around?

Dusk leaves those questions in the air.

Wolf Seven Fifty-Five.

CHAPTER 10

The Hunter is a Lonely Heart

Rick's radio informs him that Seven Fifty-Five has been detected way down, west of Lamar Valley, about seven miles from here. We go. Walking to a low rise, we find Seven Fifty-Five's fresh tracks in the snow right around us. We think we hear one deep, resonant howl, from a heavily timbered hill east of us. I'm not sure.

Then another wolf—one of the Junction Pack—howls as if replying from a partly fog-shrouded mountainside.

Now in our scopes we can see several Junction wolves traveling along in the snow of a high timber-fringed ridge about a mile away. The Junctions' two alphas, the male Puff and his noticeably limping mate, Ragged Tail, lead two gray and three black wolves through fresh powder in bright sunlight, breaking trail while coming down a series of slopes and flat spots. "He's a good leader," Rick says without taking his eye from his scope, "He likes to stay ahead of the pack."

High on the precipice of one flat spot, overlooking expansive sage flats and the winding bison-dotted banks of Crystal Creek, the Junction wolves pause as if admiring their territory.

They throw back their heads and raise into the wide sky a minutes-long chorus. For more than an hour, they continue alternately traveling and howling—sometimes both—slowly descending, in and out of timber. Through the broad landscape they continue down, down, stopping to howl, down across open snow, howling again, into a maze of tall sage and—. Gone.

We of course pack up and travel, too. We'll wait for them about a mile away, where they should reappear. Partly because I am so cold, partly because they are out of sight, I wonder at our dogged determination to keep seeing, seeing, seeing them. Why not just feel glad we saw and heard wolves and call it a day? Why this so interests us is almost as mysterious as where they'll be next. But day by day it grows more special.

Something true is here, something real. They live with a kind of faith in themselves. They have endured. So I'm into waiting out the next sighting. Laurie says we keep at it because wolves *do* things. When wolves are doing nothing, we want to know what they will do next. She adds, "When someone says to me, 'There's a grizzly bear just down the road,' all I want to know is, 'Is there a wolf with it?'"

One *sees* bison and bighorns, but one *watches* wolves. Even the bison and bighorns watch wolves. When we are not actually watching wolves, we wait until there are wolves to watch. "When I was a classroom teacher," Laurie relates, "I loved watching the kids. How they all fit in. In elementary school some liked the sandbox, some liked chasing each other; and I watched them develop over years. That's how I look at the wolves. It's kinda the same thing. It's not just *wolves* we're following. It's wolves' *stories*."

The howling continues, off and on, wolves telling their own stories.

Suddenly, through the crystal air from the east—behind us— comes a reply more resonant and mournful than the Junction pack's chorus. Seven Fifty-Five. We don't see him. How individual and unique he sounds!

The wolf may not have the words. What they have are recognition, motivation, emotion, mental images, a mind map of their landscape, a roster of their community, a store of memories, learned skills, and a catalog of scents with meanings attached. As we see in dogs, that's easily more than enough to understand who's who and what's where, every day.

For over an hour, back and forth they keep the conversation going, taking turns or overlapping. There is a kind of story in their music, wordless but full of life.

Seven Fifty-Five is the baritone I imagined a big, howling wolf would be. So distinctive, I would recognize his voice easily tomorrow and the next day. I hear his recent tragedy in his song. But do the other wolves hear that? Am I just projecting? Or is he?

Seven Fifty-Five remains unseen, howling from a heavily timbered, heavily bouldered slope caged in slanted tree-shadows. With our scopes, we are performing a fine inspection of those shadows. I'm searching in vain when Laurie says, "Got him."

Laurie's near-supernatural powers of sight exceed her explanatory prowess. "By the big tree to the left of that boulder" is not helping me narrow my scrutiny of an entire mountainside sprouting big trees and prickled with boulders. It's easier to just look through her scope. So I step up and look in.

I see a rock in a patch of sunlight under the bough of a pine. And a silvered ruff of fur. And from that, Seven Fifty-Five suddenly materializes, as if my eyes needed a moment to paint him there, curled on a boulder with his chin resting on his front paws like a pup on a porch. Waiting for—a thought? A decision? A little company?

"How the heck did you ever see him?"

"I don't know—I just saw fur."

Seven Fifty-Five sits up on that big boulder. He's just sitting there in a patch of sunlight like a fluffy dog, looking across the valley toward the howling Junctions.

He was born black, but in his late middle years he is graying, making him two-toned from any angle, with a distinctive two-toned face: dark forehead, dark ears, dark snout, abruptly contrasting light gray from his lower jaw out to the deep fur of his wide facial ruff. He has a dark cape and dark tail but creamy-looking sides. A very distinctive wolf. He throws his head back. It takes a second or two for his howl to reach me. So he's about a third of a mile away.

He looks directly into my scope. People have told me that a wolf looks *right through* you. But you know what I realize? That's because a wolf isn't interested in you. It's always hard for humans to accept that we're not the most important thing anyone's ever seen. To him I am not significant enough to look right through. He looks right *past* me. His yellow eyes merely note me momentarily: "human." Like something useless that a fisherman throws back.

The Junction female, Jet Black, howling as she goes, moves down onto the sage flats, across the steep-cut creek bank, and into willows. This is the wolf Seven Fifty-Five was trailing yesterday, who was moving away from him.

Now the Junctions have all moved down to the valley floor, strung out with their alpha couple, Ragged Tail and Puff, leading, going in and out of view in the willows, howling occasionally.

Seven Fifty-Five remains alert to the Junctions' intermittent callings, turning his head a bit, triangulating, maintaining his fix on their precise movements in the valley.

He turns his head, seeming to look straight into my telescope. I keep my gaze on him long enough—*those eyes, that face*—that the wind makes my eyes water a little. I look away to wipe them, and when I look back into the scope, I see an empty rock. Seven Fifty-Five has vanished.

Suddenly, incredibly, he's sauntering across the same low ridge we are standing on, just two hundred yards to our left. I turn and get him square in the middle of my telephoto lens and trigger off a series of images of him nicely side-lit, his focus attentively ahead, two-toned like no other wolf I've seen. Riding his long legs at a brisk lope through the sagebrush, he's heading straight toward the willows that screen Jet Black. From our hill we can see them all. But from *his* angle on the valley floor, they are over the creek bank, out of sight.

Puff stiffens, then goes into a stalk. Puff has a silly name, but he is a survivor and, says Laurie, "He's a gutsy wolf for his size." Abruptly Puff charges into the sagebrush, running fast and hard. Seven Fifty-Five bursts from the sage into the wide open. But Puff seems to be chasing his own daughter, Jet Black, as if reprimanding her. Now he breaks off the chase.

The Junction yearlings are rallying together, tail flags flying, noses and bodies rubbing. Is all the adult maneuvering making them anxious?

It's making me anxious.

Seven Fifty-Five runs straight back in their direction. He seems determined to make contact. He submerges deep into the sagebrush. The Junctions are looking around as if they don't know where he is.

Ragged Tail's bushy tail suddenly snaps straight out behind her. She has seen him.

Seven Fifty-Five abruptly banks. He is taking a big risk. Or maybe he understands his odds. Quite likely, he is acquainted with the Junctions. Puff has earned a reputation as a wolf who avoids fighting. (That might be why he's still alive.) Still, Seven-Fifty-Five has cause for caution. But he seems determined; he needs a partner and has come here to get one. He knows who he wants. He appears conflicted between attraction and fear. And logically so. Even if Puff isn't very aggressive, Seven-Fifty-Five has no guarantees. He's outnumbered, vulnerable.

Rick comments, "If you're a male with a high degree of social intelligence, you might be able to gain a pack's acceptance through displays of submission. Or you might be able to lure an adult daughter away. These things happen." He adds, "So there are a lot of similarities between wolves and what you already know about human behavior."

Years ago, when the Druids and the Slough wolves were bitter enemies, a Druid male made friends with all the Slough pups. Then he made friends with all the adult females. "This took him some time. But he kept away from the big guy. When the big guy came toward him, he would kind of tuck his tail and walk away, showing he was no threat at all and withdrawing." Later, when the big guy approached, he stayed put but rolled onto his back, then licked the big guy's face." And that worked. "If he had played it differently, he might have been killed."

We would not guess that a wolf could have a long-term social strategy, Rick acknowledges. "But when you actually watch them day after day, year after year, the best-fitting explanations are that they can have a strategy, that they sometimes do, and that outcomes depend on how individual personalities play their hand, in a sense. You never really know what to expect."

*　*　*

Seven Fifty-Five is suddenly face-to-face with the matriarch Ragged Tail atop the creek-bank bluff. No aggression. And where's Puff? Will he come and attack? He has to realize that Seven Fifty-Five is meeting his mate.

It's hard to suppress the impression that Seven Fifty-Five is greeting the lady of the house like a nervous young man before a date with her daughter. Seven Fifty-Five and Jet Black seem mutually interested in each other but keep a distance. I think they've previously met. Laurie calls her Miss Personality, but at just under two years old, she is on the lowest rung of the Junctions' female ladder.

So Jet Black's decision is high stakes: She'll either leave her parents and siblings and try to breed—with a single male who has no pack and no territory—or stay, remain low-status, and basically live to help her parents. The key word is "live."

To my amazement, Seven Fifty-Five and Jet Black mingle momentarily. It's very brief; the two alphas show themselves immediately, and their mere appearance is like showing Seven Fifty-Five the door. Puff and Ragged Tail seem interested in keeping their pack under some semblance of control. It doesn't serve them to lose a pack member.

Seven Fifty-Five returns into the maze of snowy sage. I wonder how he's feeling. I know this isn't the end of the story.

CHAPTER 11

A Will to Live

One morning during the third week of March, while springtime has decided to sleep in at *minus* seventeen degrees Fahrenheit, Doug McLaughlin sees an explosion of wolves chasing Eight-Twenty. The biggest Hoodoo male and Eight-Twenty's domineering big sister are in it. Butterfly is there. But it isn't brutal like before. Most crucially, though, reconciliation isn't in the cards. Eight-Twenty tries to follow, but they reject her again.

The next day Eight-Twenty is way west, over at Tower Junction, eating from a carcass killed by the Junction wolves. Risky. Eight-Twenty has never been there before. She appears to be scent-tracking her father. He's gone to Hellroaring.

The Lamars go in the opposite direction, east, out of the park to where the Hoodoos had come from, into that strange and imaginary place of real dangers the humans call Wyoming.

During March's final week, Eight-Twenty is still occasionally beeping in from the western part of the park. Seven-Fifty-Five is still investing a lot of time wooing Jet Black from the outskirts of the Junction Pack and dodging Puff. Meanwhile, Puff seems content to just chase. Everyone says he isn't one to fight; apparently, he isn't.

In early April, hundreds of elk begin returning to the park. A bit perplexingly, Seven-Fifty-Five has been hanging with a new, unfamiliar female, who seems to return to him some youthful vigor. They play on a snow slope and slide all the way down. "Whoever she is," comments Laurie, "she's a frisky one."

Meanwhile, Eight-Twenty has fallen in with her older sister, Middle Gray, and a huge new gray male. Middle Gray, formerly living a reduced-status life under her domineering littermate, has never shown any aggression to Eight-Twenty. She's got one of her black sisters with her, but when that sister starts to bully Eight-Twenty, Middle Gray slams her to the ground and stands over her. Is Middle Gray seeing herself as a new alpha? Is the Lamar Pack coming apart?

This could work out for Eight-Twenty. Yet reason doesn't entirely rule the decisions of wolves or people. And maybe that black sister just won't cut it out. At any rate, it isn't long before Eight-Twenty is gone again.

She travels back westward alone, miles and miles. And over near Hellroaring she finds her father, with his new female. The new female probably treats Eight-Twenty as a rival. The next day, Eight-Twenty is missing.

Why can't this family get along? They did—before hunters shot up the pack.

At Slough, a group of elk are pointed like weather vanes at seven wolves coming through a gap. The Lamar wolves are back. The bigger of the Hoodoos, known as Tall, quickens his pace. One of the black two-year-old sisters starts running in the opposite direction. Next, one elk, separated, is running hard across the flats toward the water. Behind the elk, a black streak is steadily gaining. It's a long chase. The black wolf grabs the elk by its hock and hangs on while being whipped up and down like a fluttering leaf. The elk makes it to the creek just as the other wolves converge. Some very wet wolves accomplish their task.

In a surprise appearance, Middle Gray suddenly emerges, looking pregnant—and gets a very warm greeting from all the Lamar wolves. Where is her huge new male? What's going on? Six months ago, the Lamars were a stable group. Now the membership is continually changing.

April 18 delivers a steely minus five degrees Fahrenheit with a spiteful wind. Winter seems to have its jaws locked on Yellowstone's throat. Yet heeding internal alarm clocks, grizzly moms with new cubs are emerging from hibernation, showing themselves here and there. Pronghorn "antelope" are back up in Lamar Valley.

The Lamars slow their trot to look at a newborn bison. It would seem easy, but bison seem to have their own sense of life and death, and like most people, they prefer life. The small band of bison adults charges the wolves, easily routing them. Doug tells me that sometimes bison even have "funerals" involving solemn group inspection of a fallen comrade. I never knew.

Meanwhile, Laurie wants to rename Puff, calling him Hunter instead. Since hunting is what wolves do, I don't think Hunter is a very distinguishing name for a wolf. So I'll let Laurie tell you what she just saw him do:

"Puff split an elk herd that had started to run, and picked out a healthy yearling. The elk was already probably twice Puff's weight and was running like a rocket. But Puff was pouring on extra speed, closing the gap. He briefly got a throat hold, then a leg hold, but two adult female elk came to its defense; one seemed to trample Puff. This let the yearling bolt. It put a lot of distance between itself and him. At that point the elk should have escaped. But incredibly, Puff ran a wide circle around those other elk and followed the one he'd attacked. Again he poured on extra speed and was soon beside the galloping yearling elk. Puff lunged and latched onto the elk's throat, but the yearling elk was strong and had no intention of going down. Puff then bodychecked the elk while applying a violent twist, and the elk stumbled and fell. Puff's pack caught up and all ate heavily. Puff is not a large wolf. But having survived a ravaging mange that gave him his name, he has turned into a relentless and seriously effective hunter."

In May, Seven Fifty-Five and Eight-Twenty seem to be taking turns sending beeps from Mount Everts, near the park's northwest border. Father and daughter seem to have reunited. But they don't seem to be spending their time together. Likely Eight-Twenty can't get along comfortably with Dad's new mate. Eight-Twenty drifts north, out of the park.

Meanwhile, the Lamars' Middle Gray has pups, in the old Druid Pack den. No one has seen the pups but she's obviously nursing, and her mate and her black sister have been hauling plenty of food up toward the den site. The rest of what was once the Lamars are out east of the park again in Wyoming, where the Hoodoo males are from.

Someone has the courtesy to share on Facebook that "Middle Gray would make a nice rug." The bullying taunts show that shooting wolves isn't just hunting. It's acting out some people's desire to inflict pain not just on wolves but on other people, people who aren't like themselves.

By July, Eight-Twenty is fairly stationary, outside the park near Jardine, Montana. To a wolf like Eight-Twenty, who has known people and roads all her life, Jardine offers plenty of opportunities for misunderstandings.

THE BILLINGS GAZETTE. August 26.

```
  1 HOUR AGO—A young collared female gray
wolf was shot by a Jardine-area resident
on Saturday after the wolf had recently
come in close proximity to a number of
homes. . . . It was shot while eating a
chicken.
```

Having dined on a few chickens myself, I pause to ponder getting shot for doing so. The article notes:

```
  All together, hunters . . . shot 12 wolves
last year that spent part of their time
inside Yellowstone's boundaries. Six of the
12 wolves were collared.
```

So ends the sad ballad of Eight-Twenty, a precocious, talented wolf in her prime, who, in a better world, might have matured to lead a worthy wolf enterprise. She never quite learned—despite the killings of her uncle and her famous mother—that humans can be murder.

On a happy note—if you like wolves, and I do—Seven Fifty-Five is finally keeping steady company with Jet Black. She was the lowest-ranking Junction wolf. As an underdog, she seems worth rooting for. When they greet, they are all over each other with wagging tails and happiness. Amid such death and tragedy, there is in their daily ritual a genuinely redemptive quality of renewal. We all feel it.

Though the catastrophe that befell Seven Fifty-Five and his pack the previous autumn seemed to suggest that his life was over, he would be a survivor. Two years after he lost his mate, his brother, his pack, and his territory, I finished this book. And on the day I did, I logged in to Laurie Lyman's Yellowstone reports. And there he was. Seven Fifty-Five, still alive and well, having proven himself a survivor against all odds. It made me remember a point Doug Smith had made emphatically. "Wolves are tough," he'd told me. "Very—*tough.*"

Eight-Twenty having a rough time with two of her sisters.

Jude, Carl Safina, and a stick-biting Chula.

CHAPTER 12

Domestic Servants

Wolves' personalities, abilities, and social dynamics make me think of them as dogs who get the chance to grow up and take charge of their own lives. They have their own families; their own social order, politics, and ambitions; they make their own decisions and earn their livings. They are full captains of their lives, sometimes cruel and violent with one another; often friendly, loyal, supportive. They know who to protect and who to attack. They're their own masters, their own best friends. Always unleashed. No food bowls. They have freedom, and with freedom comes hazard. Wolves have plenty of both. They're always playing for keeps.

The similarity with dogs runs deep because all dogs are domesticated wolves. I'll explain. One super-important thing before we proceed: "Domesticated" means genetically changed from wild ancestors by selective breeding. One way to think of it: Zoos have wild animals in captivity; farms have domesticated animals. Arboretums have wild plants; farms have domesticated plants. "Domesticated" doesn't mean tame. A wolf that was captive-born and bottle-raised and is entirely tame is a wolf in captivity; it's not *domesticated*. Pet parrots, even captive-bred, are not domesticated.

Domestication implies intentional human creation of animal and plant varieties or breeds that don't exist in nature. Classically, that's accomplished by selective breeding. Now technicians often use genetic engineering. Farmers, fanciers, and researchers select traits they want. They breed individuals with those traits, resulting in many varieties of domestic chickens, cows, pigs, pigeons, laboratory rats, rat terriers, farmed salmon, corn, rice, wheat, and so on, all genetically changed from their nature-evolved, wild-type ancestors.

Dogs make domestication *very* interesting. Dogs *may* be the only creatures ever to have domesticated themselves. Except—we might have domesticated ourselves, too.

So, all dogs were domesticated from free-living gray wolves. Their domestication occurred, at most, just a few times—maybe only once— by about 15,000 years ago. All dogs are a domestic *variety* of wolf. A highly *variable* variety. Outwardly, many dogs look so different from wolves that scientists first assumed dogs were a different species. In 1758, the domestic dog was given a Latin name, *Canis familiaris*. Gray wolves are called *Canis lupus*. And obviously, dog breeds—greyhounds, mastiffs, dachshunds—are genetically different from one another. But as scientists peer into dogs' DNA, they've realized that while the visual differences are major—genetic changes are tiny. One can argue over the definition of "species" (many do). But very little has changed *genetically* between wolf and domestic dog. So little, in fact, that scientists have changed dogs' Latin name back to wolf, back to *Canis lupus,* telling us who they were before we adopted them, who they really are. Dogs are now *Canis lupus familiaris.* Wolf. But *familiaris* says they are *our* wolf. The communicative postures we see in dogs—the crouching invitation to play; the submissive rolling onto their backs, tails between legs; and the loyalty—these are wolf behaviors that survive in the domesticated wolves we live with.

When people first realized that dogs are direct descendants of gray wolves, they imagined Stone Age people finding wolf pups and bringing them into caves as the first pets. But as best we know now, the origin of dogs goes like this instead: Wolves hung around human camps and caves, scrounging cast-off bones and the remains of butchered carcasses. The less skittish wolves came closer and got more. Wolves with fuller bellies raised more pups, born carrying those successful genes for less skittishness. Those slightly changed pups grew up around humans, prompting more and friendlier interactions.

These wolves' tendency to alert at the approach of strangers and predators would have been valuable. By providing more scraps, the humans would encourage such guards to hang around. The extra scraps would boost survival of more people-friendly wolf pups.

This went on for centuries. These human-oriented wolves

specialized in exploiting humans as a new resource. Human camps were a new habitat. Friendlies got the most food. Eventually they were regulars around camps, began guarding human camps as their territories, and began to follow on human hunts. Those friendly genes proliferated.

So researchers now believe that's how the first dogs happened; by coming near human camps, wolves unintentionally *domesticated themselves* to humans.

But that first unintended domestication wasn't entirely one-way. Because dogs received survival advantages, dogs evolved to be oriented toward humans. And because humans received survival advantages from dogs, we became oriented toward dogs. As our unique emotional response to their wagging tails whispers, they domesticated us a bit, too.

Dogs pick up on human cues, such as pointing, in a way that even chimpanzees, surprisingly, do not. Wolves, too, can follow human pointing to find hidden food—without being trained to do so. After all, free-living wolves must be finely attuned to where one another's attention is directed. Dogs understand fully where humans' attention is focused, so if you throw a ball and turn away, your dog will bring the ball around to where you're facing.

Humans, meanwhile, became very dog-oriented. But did humans actually *evolve* an orientation toward dogs? I think of it this way: Is there anything a cow, chicken, bunny, goat, or pig does with its body that gives you the same feeling you get from seeing a dog's tail wagging?

Of course, some people don't like dogs. Some love the purr of a cat or the sight of a pig. But many people feel their dogs' bond as part of the family's. Humans' moods match dogs' moods more intimately; many people seem to experience more emotional contagion—in other words, more empathy—with dogs than with any other species.

So I think, yes, to a certain extent, humans and dogs might have co-evolved. Humans became dog-reliant, perhaps even dog-dependent. Dogs were trackers and hunting aides; dogs were alarm systems and well-armed guards; dogs defended and played with human children. Dogs cleaned up. Dogs were hot-water bottles. Humans provided dogs with food, and dogs served as security personnel and guides. And helped us hunt for food, too.

Once we had them, they had us; we could not do without them. People brought dogs to the far ends of the earth. It's likely that hunting peoples would not have penetrated the high Arctic without them. In the Far North, dogs were transportation, freight haulers, and in the toughest times, dogs became food. Dogs went to Australia, too (where, faced with a new continent and no competitors, some re-wilded, becoming dingoes). Dogs came across the Bering Sea to the Americas. In *Empire of the Summer Moon,* S. C. Gwynne writes of an 1860 army attack on a Comanche camp: "In the midst of the struggle, the white soldiers found themselves under attack from fifteen or so dogs from the Indian camp, who tried valiantly to defend their Indian masters. Almost all were shot and killed." The dogs' loyalties and self-identities made them war combatants. Dogs seem to be wherever people are. I once visited Papua

New Guinea to work on sea turtles. On that wild coast, tiny villages of just twenty to eighty inhabitants were separated from one another by distances requiring hours of walking. Yet each village had several dogs hanging around, living off scraps—as their ancestors had started doing tens of thousands of years earlier.

Thousands of years later, we're still uncovering dogs' hidden abilities. At least one border collie responds to an unfamiliar word by choosing the unfamiliar object. At the command "Get the dax!" the dog apparently reasons along these lines: *There's a ball here, but she didn't ask for ball. "Dax" must mean this other thing that I've never seen before.* Such skills of inference, write the scientists who studied this, "have only been demonstrated previously for language learning in human children."

Even dogs aren't the best at everything, though. Apes are good at finding hidden food by, for instance, seeing a board tilted up, indicating the presence of something under it. Dogs are terrible at that. (That's a visual cue; dogs excel at searching by smell.) Ravens—the wolf birds—are good at figuring out which of several crossed strings is connected to the treat. Primates do those tasks easily. Dogs are terrible at this, too. (Again, it's purely visual.)

But a raven probably couldn't guide a blind person across the street or warn you of an oncoming seizure. Dogs can do this in stride, with pride.

Wolves are social, and humans are *enormously* social. Dogs can depend on us because both they and we are social enough to understand one another. Depending on humans, though, comes with costs (as we all know). Dependence costs freedom, self-sufficiency, and a sense of self-reliance. When dogs and wolves are presented with a locked box containing food, the dogs almost immediately stop trying and start looking back and forth from the human to the box, as if thinking, *Can you help me?* Wolves keep trying to solve the task until the test times out. Wolves perform as well as or better than dogs on practical problem solving and memory tasks.

Dogs' social skills are their wolf heritage, but dogs' *orientation to humans* resulted from domestication.

Chula shaking off right after a swim.

So we're at a strange place in a unique relationship: Dogs domesticated themselves. Not *only* did dogs domesticate themselves, but dogs domesticated humans, too. In becoming reliant on us, they made us reliant on them. We became like one another.

During dogs' ancient first domestication, many of the genes that changed in wolves that were becoming dogs are *the same* genes that were changing in humans, too. For instance, as humans and their dogs transitioned from being mainly hunters to living in farming cultures, they and we both evolved genes to help ease the digestion and metabolism of starches.

Dogs' friendliness results from their genetically altered brain chemistry. Ours does, too. In both dogs and humans, we went from being wanderers to living in towns. Living in increasingly crowded conditions made it important to reduce aggression. "Humans have had to tame themselves," says Adam Boyko of Cornell University, adding, "Similar to dogs, you have to tolerate the presence of others."

Serotonin, a chemical made by the body, can make people feel happier and less tense. (It does many other things, too.) Both dogs and humans have the same gene controlling a protein that transports serotonin. Serotonin researchers have learned so much about mood disorders from serotonin in dogs that they concluded, "Our best friend in the animal kingdom might provide us with one of the most enchanting systems for our understandings of human evolution and disease."

It would seem that wolves, as our canine companions, have come to join in the human conversation in surprising ways. And remarkably, we understand one another pretty doggone well.

———— ∞ ————

But why did dogs start *looking* less like wolves and more like dogs? Turns out—and no one could have predicted this, and no one did— the same genes that make animals friendly toward humans also affect *physical* traits. Weirdly, in various mammals (not just dogs), genes that create the hormones that reduce fear and aggression and increase friendliness *also* create floppy ears, curly tails, blotchy markings, shorter faces, and rounder heads.

Though he didn't understand why (genes were unknown in his time), Charles Darwin noted, "Not a single domestic animal can be named which has not in some country drooping ears." Now, floppy ears are *not* found in *any* wild animal adult. But don't we just love floppy ears? Some of the traits that humans find so endearing and huggable in dogs are exactly the ones that come along, by sheer coincidence, with a genetically caused tendency for friendliness.

Our emotional response to those floppy ears is as if *our own* friendly feelings toward dogs did indeed co-evolve with theirs toward us, so that we experience a positive emotional response to animals who *look* most friendly. They *are* most friendly. And as I've mentioned, how about our instant response to that wagging tail? Humans and dogs, it appears, learned to love one another in deep, genetic ways. It sure can feel that way.

How do we know that friendliness, floppy ears, and a curled tail are tangled genetically? To explain, we need to bring in the famous Russian foxes.

In 1959, scientists in Siberia began a decades-long experiment into the genetic basis of behavior. To see whether friendliness has a genetic basis, they set up two populations of captive foxes. One population bred randomly. In the other population, only foxes who acted less aggressive, less fearful, and friendlier to humans were allowed to breed. The researchers were interested *only* in aggression—not looks.

They got more than they bargained for.

Over several generations—faster than expected—the selectively bred foxes got friendlier. But what really surprised the scientists—and everyone else—is that from generation to generation, the line of friendlier foxes started to *look* different. Researchers were getting foxes with droopy ears; splotchy coats that could be straight-haired or kinky; curling, wagging tails; shorter legs; smaller heads with smaller brains; and shorter faces with smaller teeth. And some showed behavior associated with breeding when it was not breeding season. As adults, the friendly foxes continued to behave like juveniles, by acting submissive, whining, and giving higher-pitched barks. Foxes, in other words, became more like dogs. (The randomly breeding foxes continued to both look and act like wild foxes.)

The friendly foxes had reduced levels of hormones involved in fear and defensiveness. It's not surprising that foxes born friendlier have different brain chemical activity than foxes who are fearful and defensive with people. They would have to, because brain chemicals create behavioral tendencies and moods.

So—genes resulting in invisible brain changes for friendly behavior *also* result in changes in how foxes look. The scientists did not care how the foxes looked; they selected *only* for friendly behavior. The changed looks came along for the ride, tangled into the effects of the same genes that result in friendliness.

Some researchers call the whole set of traits that come hitchhiking on friendliness genes "domestication syndrome." Among the controlled chaos of DNA are multitasking efficiencies such that the *same* hormone—dopamine, say—that affects mood might *also* affect hair color.

Researchers and farmers might have *thought* that they were selecting for mellow personalities, but they were really selecting for juvenile-style adults. They were creating perpetual pups. Cows and pigs, goats, rabbits—similar physical changes came along with mellow tempers. The human breeder says, "Don't bite," but the genome hears, "Never grow up." So maybe a better name than domestication syndrome would be Peter Pan syndrome.

Jude seems deep in thought. We call him "the poet."

So, some wolves seem to have self-domesticated into dogs. And in the process they domesticated us to them. And none of this was planned; it just happened. That means that simply preventing aggressive individuals from breeding can eventually get you a population of more juvenile-like adults. This seems true for other animals. How about for us?

Romping at the beach. Jude above, Chula below.

CHAPTER 13

Two Ends of the
Same Leash

Researchers Brian Hare and Michael Tomasello suggest that, just maybe, "an important first step in the evolution of modern human societies was a kind of self-domestication."

Hare and Tomasello, recalling those Russian foxes in which only the friendly ones were allowed to breed and make more friendly foxes, speculated that early humans, "either killed or drove away those people who were overly aggressive."

Well, killing overly aggressive people doesn't sound like a great path to friendliness. But isn't taming our aggressiveness the main story of the struggle for human freedom and dignity? Aren't we always searching for peace, always seeking more perfect ways of taming ourselves, of behaving in ways we can call civil? Self-domestication does indeed seem part of the human program. The process of becoming more civil is called civilization.

*   *   *

Experimental foxes, our family dogs; all show that along for the ride with genes that boost friendliness come physical changes, programmed into the same stretches of DNA. We can see it in other domesticated animals. Over many generations of domestication, most mammals (cows, pigs, sheep, goats, even guinea pigs) actually got smaller, with slenderized skeletons compared to their more robust free-living ancestral relatives. Typically the skull's braincase becomes smaller, as does the brain itself. The muzzle shortens, causing relative flattening of the face. This creates tooth crowding, and teeth themselves become smaller. Size differences between males and females narrow. Hair colors and textures diversify. Fat-storage capacity increases under the skin and in muscle. Activity decreases. Docility increases. Juvenile behaviors, including play and reduced levels of male aggression, extend into adulthood.

During domestication, dogs lost as much as 30 percent of brain size relative to body weight compared to wolves. Pigs and ferrets, about the same; mink about 20 percent, horses about 15 percent. Domestic guinea pigs are less interested in aggression and less interested in the environment around them compared to wild ones, called cavies. Genetic changes during the process of selection and domestication cause these differences.

Thousands of years ago, as people became more numerous and began the long process toward settled living, similar physical changes appeared in some human populations. According to American anthropologist Osbjorn Pearson, around 130,000 years ago, the first modern humans "had much smaller faces" than Neanderthals' faces. We tend to assume that civilization made humans larger, but earlier humans actually shrank. By about 18,000 years ago, people in Europe had lost about four inches of height. This trend continued during the transition to agriculture thousands of years later. During that time, humans and their domesticated animals *all* began to show reductions in size, shortening of the face and jaws, and smaller and more crowded teeth. Improvements in health and nutrition over the last two hundred years have finally made Europeans as tall as their Paleolithic ancestors.

We also have smaller brains than did Neanderthals. Our modern brains, with a volume of about 1,350 cubic centimeters, are smaller than the 1,500-cubic-centimeter brain formerly possessed by Neanderthals. Such physical changes generally accelerated with the spread of farming.

Animals under early domestication received shelter, a diet altered by agriculture, and protection from predators. This reduced their sensory needs, facilitating further domestication. As our domesticated animals settled in for a life of reduced activity and reduced stimulation, so did humans. As people provided safer, more sedentary conditions for their livestock, they did the same for themselves. The confinement was mutual.

By moving out of nature and settling on farms, we became in a real sense another type of farm animal. Caltech brain researcher John Allman says that humans domesticated themselves. We now depend on others to provide food and shelter. We're a lot like poodles in that regard.

Cows and goats don't seem very alert to their surroundings; they don't have to be. And neither do the people who keep them. Archaeologist Colin Groves writes, "Humans have undergone a reduction in environmental awareness in parallel to domestic species and for exactly the same reason." Security has cost us a certain dulling of senses.

We tend to think that humans evolved, then stopped evolving and started culture. What's clear is—that is wrong. Farming and civilization were enormous changes in the human environment, massively altering selective pressures. Pressures to maintain a hunter's size and strength and senses relaxed, while pressure to behave cooperatively, expand social skills, and suppress violent urges intensified. Small, slender, thin-boned people might not have excelled at the rigors of mammoth hunting. But people requiring fewer calories might have survived better during crop failures. The point is this: As the pressures change, we remain a work in progress.

Look at the evolving creature in the mirror. Realize that we've got a way to go before we're as loyal to one another as our dogs are to us.

———

It's been said that no species are more alike than wolves and humans. If you watch wolves not just in all their beauty and adaptability but in all their brutality, it's hard to escape the conclusion that we have a lot in common with wolves.

Living as we do in family packs, fending off the human wolves among us, managing the wolves within us, we can easily recognize in real wolves their social dilemmas and their quests for status.

Consider the similarities between male wolves and men. They're quite striking. Males of very few species *directly* enhance the survival of females or young year-round. For example, most male birds provide food to females and young only during the breeding season. In a few fishes and a few monkey species, males actively care for young, but only while young are small. Owl monkey males carry and protect babies, but they don't feed them. Male lemurs challenge predators, enabling females to escape, but they don't provide any food.

Helping get food year-round, bringing food to babies, helping raise young to full maturity over several years, *and* defending females and offspring against strangers who threaten their safety is a very rare package to find in a male. Human males and wolf males—that's about it. And the more dependably faithful of the two—isn't us. Male wolves more reliably stick with the program, helping raise young *and* actually helping females survive.

Chimpanzees are closer relatives, and we look much more like chimps than we look like wolves. But male chimps don't help feed babies or bring food back to a homesite. Wolves and humans can understand each other better. That's one reason why we invited wolves, not chimpanzees, into our lives. Wolves and dogs and us: It's not surprising that we found each other. We deserve one another. We were made for each other.

I've explained that thousands of years ago, the beginning of the story of dogs started with wolves who hung around human camps, scrounging cast-off food and gnawing leftover bones. I get a daily reminder of this while preparing dinner, as I look down to see our doggies Chula and Jude looking up at me, waiting for scraps and leftovers. Or I glance at our living room floor and see them chewing bone treats we've given them. Really, in tens of thousands of years, the basics of the relationship haven't changed much. But they have certainly deepened and grown stronger.

In our kitchens, on our floors and sofas, in our laps, and in our beds, hidden in plain sight among humans who've forgotten the ancient origins of our eager pets, wolves in dogs' clothing riddle our homes and transform our families and our hearts, wagging their sweet tails, being our working partners and best friends. It's not as ironic as it might seem that a creature as violent as a wolf could domesticate itself into becoming humanity's most beloved companion. In the form of their dog avatar, wolves mesh with humans through their keen instinctive grasp of in-group, out-group living. A wolf knows who to protect and who to attack and how to defend to the death.

That obsession for distinguishing friend from foe is one we share. It's why we understand one another on the one hand and fear one another on the other. It's why, since deep antiquity, we have viewed wolves as everything from guards to gods.

To watch wild wolves is to recognize a kindred creature. They are riveting, horrifying, and admirable. You watch them and you see that many of our dogs' tendencies and talents were fully formed in the wild and remain intact in our homes.

Dogs have been diversified into an enormous range; think of Great Danes and Chihuahuas. Yet a dog seems to recognize at a distance the difference between another dog—no matter what the breed—and a cat. And so do children.

Rick McIntyre likes to tell people that "because many households have dogs, we already know about both."

"You mean both wolves and dogs? Or both wolves and humans?" I ask.

"Right," he says.

"Does my dog love me, or does she just want a treat?" A professor who is an expert in climate change—not dogs—recently asked me that question. I've often asked it myself. Short answer: Your dog really does love you. Part of the reason is that you are kind. If you were abusive, your dog would fear you. And your dog might *still* love you out of duty or need—not so different from people.

But to answer the question directly: What we know about dogs' brains, their brain chemistry, and the changes to their brains caused by domestication tells us that, yes, your dog loves you. A dog's ability to feel love for humans comes partly from the love wolves have for wolves, partly from the genetic changes of their domesticated ancestry.

In dogs, we've bred the people we wish we could be: loyal, hard-working, watchful, fiercely protective, intuitive, sensitive, affectionate, helpful to those in need. No matter how their feelings originated, they are real to dogs. Your dog genuinely loves you, as you, in your domesticated state, activating the deep, old parts of your brain, love your dog.

———◦———

Just outside Bozeman, Montana, Chris Bahn and his wife Mary-Martha run a bed-and-breakfast called Howlers Inn. In fenced acres right next to their home, they provide for several captive-born wolves who needed a haven. Chris and Mary-Martha raised these wolves by hand, bottle-feeding them from the age of three weeks. They are real wolves, not wolf-dog hybrids. They've known no other life. When I drove up, they came to the fence like dogs, curious.

Having read about the rare friendly foxes with the curly tails and theories that friendly wolves domesticated themselves—which all made perfect sense—I was nonetheless unprepared for the first time I saw a man interact with tame, undomesticated wolves.

When Chris entered the enclosure, he was wearing a canvas jumpsuit to protect himself from the enthusiasm of their surprisingly long and sharp claws. What surprised me most, though, was their doglike friendliness. They were wagging their tails, happily rallying around him. (I had to remain outside.)

Chris Bahn and the tame wolves at Howlers Inn.

"Wolves are extremely expressive," Chris says, looking up at me while kneeling in a sea of swarming wolves. "Probably even more so than dogs. You always know whether they're happy or relaxed or uncomfortable."

The alpha male, aged six, came for vigorous rubs and then rolled belly-up. Chris crouched down and obliged, while others gave him licks to the face, just as Jude likes to do while I'm rubbing Chula's belly at home. I asked Chris where he is in the pack order. He says he's not; he has no dominance role. His role is caretaker.

Seeing these wolves, it made perfect sense that wolves acquired a habit of hanging around human habitations thousands of years ago and then, as centuries came and went, fit better and better into the human social structure. For wolves, changing into dogs would have been a good career move.

CHAPTER 14

Pet Peeves

In the morning I'm making coffee, and because it's chilly I close some windows. The phone rings and I answer it. Chula follows all my movement, looking me in the eyes for any clues that I might wish to interact—or perhaps move toward the jar of treats. Or my car keys. She does not understand coffee, windows, or phones. Any human from most of our species' history, or a Native American in 1880, or a member of a remaining hunter-gatherer tribe today also would not understand anything I was doing. The difference between my lovable dog and any human is that any human could have learned everything I am doing. My dog will never fully understand what I'm up to most mornings. But, again, the point is not whether dogs are just like us. The point is that they are like themselves. The interesting question is, what are they like?

We grab the car keys, and Chula and Jude get excited. I open the door and say "car," and they run for the car's back hatch.

At the river, we let them out. They love this, of course. A swan sees them running along the shore. He steps into the water, paddling just out of easy reach. The dogs go into the water up to their bellies and bark at the swan a few times. The swan is actually stemming the current in place, not paddling away, not even drifting away. Either he doesn't want to move from this point along the shore, or he's taunting them. It seems this guy is taunting the dogs. But why would he? I don't know why he's stemming and holding right there—but he must know. Is this his idea of fun?

Chula is weighing her option of swimming to the swan. You can see her trying to figure out what to do next. She wades deep enough to

Jude looking at the world on a snowy day.

almost float but seems to understand that this won't work for her. The swan clearly understands this won't work for Chula, because he is staring directly at her from just a few strokes away, not moving one feather farther. In a minute the dogs realize that this is not going to get any more fun for them, and they splash to shore and gambol off.

The swan just showed that he understood he needed to avoid the dogs, *and* he understood the limitations of their movement in water. He understood how to use the water to stay completely safe while holding himself so close that, were he on land, the dogs could cover the distance in two bounds, in half a second. The swan demonstrated that he has a mind and that his mind understands that the dogs have a mind with different goals from his, and he showed his masterful use of the water. I'm impressed.

Farther down the shore, Chula bounds into the water near where some mallard ducks are floating. They, too, paddle to deeper water but do not fly. A few hundred yards farther along the shore, the river enters Long Island Sound. The river mouth is perhaps a hundred yards across. Out in midriver, several hundred scaup—another kind of duck—are diving for mussels. They ignore the dogs. But when four humans appear on the far shore, all the ducks fly up in alarm, leaving the vicinity of the river and flying out over the Sound. As they overfly other sitting groups of scaup and long-tailed ducks, those ducks also take flight and head out over the Sound in a wide-spreading panic.

Why would the ducks merely paddle away from their age-old enemy the wolf (in domesticated form), yet become panicked by the mere appearance of humans on a farther shore? Because the ducks understand a dog's limits and have also learned that humans can kill at great distance; that's why. The ducks know that causing harm can be on a human's mind, they have some concept of danger, and they can feel fear. And because for millions of years of evolution they had no experience of guns, their accurate judgment about what constitutes differing safe distances from dogs and humans is learned, not instinctive. That's part of what's so interesting. Duck-hunting season has just ended. It's likely that all of them, even the young ones hatched last spring, have had some experience with human hunters by now.

When we get home, I towel off Chula, whose fur is full of sand, damp with brackish water. She endures it but doesn't love it. Yet as soon as I unfurl the towel, Jude dives headlong into it, tail wagging widely as he snaps his jaws randomly while prancing like a terry-cloth ghost. Jude loves playing blindman's buff. The game is to grab and release his muzzle while he's blindly snapping. Take the towel off and he stops snapping and tries to get into the towel again. Chula has no interest in this game, or in Jude when he's being so silly.

Later, in the yard surrounding our house, our dogs chase each other in play. They fake each other out when chasing around the shed or cottage. Chula tries to double back to intercept Jude, but Jude stops to see from which way Chula is coming. They know what is going on, and they seem to understand that the other is trying to fool them. One is evaluating what the other is thinking, each showing clear understanding that the other might be faked into a false belief about which direction they'll be charging from. Because they're playing, there's both cleverness and humor in this.

Knowing that another being has a mind, and that their agenda can differ from yours, is called having a theory of mind. Until very recently, many scientists who study behavior and psychology believed that only humans have this capacity to recognize that others, too, have a mind. But if you look at many animals, especially free-living animals and freely interacting doggies, you can see that *many* species require a theory of mind to judge danger and stay safe. Or to have fun.

A dog who has never before seen a ball would not bring it to a person and lay it at their feet. But a dog experienced with balls and the game of fetch comes to invite play. Dogs envision the game, plan a way to start it, and carry out their plan with human partners whom they understand can understand what they are doing. They bring the ball. And you throw it. Sometimes they keep bringing it until you need to do something else!

Any dog who goes into a play-bow is inviting you, understanding that you might engage. Dogs and others don't play-bow to trees, chairs, or other inanimate objects. Our puppy Emi play-bowed to the first ball she ever saw when I rolled it her way. She assumed anything moving so directly along the floor had to be alive—but she did that only once. In moments she realized that this was a wonderful new thing but that it was inanimate, not capable of an aware response or voluntary play. It therefore needed no further invitation, nor consideration, nor restraint in being chewed, flung, and pounced on.

Chula once barked at a life-sized concrete dog, but only once—a sniff told her that its shape had lied. A dog, or elephant, say, often validates the authenticity of things by scent. A dog who loves chasing rabbits will give a single sniff to a porcelain rabbit. It obviously recognizes rabbits on sight but is too clever to be fooled by a fake. To a dog, if it looks like a duck, and quacks like a duck, it's not a duck unless it *smells* like a duck.

These little stories reveal the dogs' shrewd ability to discern what has a mind—and what doesn't. It's happening all around us. Go outside, watch, and have some fun.

Jude, left, and Chula. Looking ferocious but just playin' on a snowy day

Jude trying hard to catch Chula.

CHAPTER 15

They're Not Confused; We're Confused

Our two young dogs came from the shelter in springtime. They grew up during summer, and all during the warm weather they could come and go from the house at will through a propped-open door. They almost never had to ask to be let out. On very rare occasions when the door was closed and they were inside, wanting out, they'd stand by the door; they never barked to be let out. They'd go out for the last time at about ten P.M., then come up to the bedroom, where they'd bed for the night on their floor beds. They would rest well until first light, when they'd get active and wake us up.

During October of their first year, we were out one evening later than we'd expected, and we fed them unusually late. Disrupted from their usual schedule, at four A.M. they got the urge to go and went downstairs to the door. I became aware of their need because one of them barked several times. They'd *never* barked to be let out before;

they never had to. Why would they bark now? They apparently understood that we were upstairs, asleep, and that, having found the door closed downstairs, they needed to get our attention. So they sent a message that we received and understood; that's the definition of communication.

The first time my wife, Patricia, drove separately with the dogs to our cottage near the beach, I had been there several days. When she arrived, Chula did a double-take at the sight of my car and immediately went to the car looking for me. I'd gone for a walk, but Chula ran excitedly into each room of the house, hoping—it seemed to Patricia—to find and greet me.

Even Chula—smart as she is—cannot talk. Communicate, yes. But talk, no. "When we ask things of animals, they often understand us," animal expert Elizabeth Marshall Thomas wrote. "When they ask things of us, we are often baffled." So we try to be better at understanding. Orangutans can evaluate how well a human is understanding their gestures. When gestures fail, they sometimes pantomime what they would like from the human. When the human has seemed to partially understand their meaning, researchers wrote, "orangutans narrowed down their range of signals." When misunderstood, however, the orangutans came up with *new* signals. Orangutans are able to establish shared meaning—if the humans prove capable of understanding.

Shared meaning. Understanding. That's the quest. We don't always need words. And even humans don't always use words. Think of love, of the way truly important things can be communicated with open arms, fingertips, a smile—with no need of sentences and without syntax. The true power of silent intent.

You can't know what your dog is thinking—except when you can. You and your dog both know if you're about to go for a walk or get into the car; and when you're preparing to give them some leftovers, you both understand it. True, most of the time I *don't* know what they're thinking. But most of the time I don't know whether my wife is thinking about how much she loves me or what she'd like for dinner. She can tell me or show me. Otherwise I can't know what's on her mind. Love and dinner occur to our dogs, too, but a dog's ability to tell us is limited. Their ability to show us is a bit better. But they have whatever thoughts they have, regardless. And it's enough, in a few words and gestures between us, for deep affection and trust, for a shared life.

Jude is one of the sweetest dogs I've known but not the sharpest. We call him "the poet" because he always seems to be daydreaming, seldom paying attention. At least that's what I thought. One day when Chula and Jude were both very young and full of energy, I took both of them for a beach run. Halfway down the beach they sniffed a deer scent and disappeared into the woods atop a bluff. Usually they return in about five minutes. This time their absence stretched to twenty, twenty-five minutes, with me calling the whole time. I finally climbed the bluff. Calling, calling. Nothing.

Then I saw Jude back down on the beach, galloping full speed in the direction we'd been headed when they'd bolted. This was odd.

Chula is *always* ahead of Jude, and Chula is *always* the first one who comes looking for me. I called Jude and he immediately stopped and came scrambling up the vine-tangled slope as I scrambled down. On the beach, I leashed him. Now I was worried; where was Chula?

Bad possibilities included an injury, getting taken by someone who thought she was lost (she does wear a tag), a run-in with a car. Minutes peeled off the clock. No Chula. Maybe she'd gone *back* to our car. I decided I'd walk back to the car, about half a mile, and if Chula wasn't there, I'd put Jude in the car and come back. But Jude would have none of it. He resisted the change of direction. Very clearly, he wanted to keep going in the direction we'd all been headed. But was this because he was having too much fun?

Unlikely. Usually when he's had this much activity, he's ready to stay close and go home. His insistence on pressing forward was odd. Then far, far down the beach—farther than we'd *ever* walked—I saw Chula running very hard, zigzagging. What a relief. But she was running *away* from us. I called as loudly as I could and waved my arms, hoping the wind might let my voice reach her. She finally heard, and in an instant turned, saw me waving, and began running hard toward us. She must have thought that the whole time they were in the woods I'd continued walking in the same direction—as in fact I usually do when they run off briefly. Apparently, she'd returned to the beach about where she'd expected to intercept me. By how hard she was running when I saw her, it seemed that she was trying to catch up and find me. Did Jude know she was down there? Did he fear that I was going to abandon Chula? No way to know, but that's certainly how he acted.

I think the dogs knew what they were doing the whole time; I was the one who'd gotten confused.

Jude and Chula *sound* and *look* like they're battling as they growl and bite. Guests to our home have asked in alarm, "Are they fighting?" But the pupsters know they're playing, and so do we. We easily hear it because we understand their tone of growl; we're in on their joke. We understand their intent, as they obviously do. We humans don't hold a monopoly on judging subtle cues.

Some humans hunt with dogs. But humans control the situation. Dolphins, however, have controlled and contrived their own situations, using humans—and in a couple of cases seemingly training humans— to help them catch food.

In both Brazil and Mauritania, dolphins drive mullet schools toward a line of fishermen. On the coast of Brazil, the dolphins seem to have trained the fishermen; along Mauritania's shore, the fishermen seem to have trained the dolphins. Brazilian bottlenose dolphins use head- and tail-slaps *to direct the humans* about when and where the fishermen should cast their nets. Only a small proportion of the dolphins there do this, in only a couple of spots—they learn from their mothers—and the fishermen know them well enough to give them names, such as Caroba and Scooby. The dolphins nab fish that become confused or injured by the nets. Mauritanian fishermen who see a school of the fish called mullet beat the water with sticks to call bottlenose and humpbacked dolphins, who then herd the mullet against their nets and take their share. They've been in business together since 1847. Most extraordinarily, for about a hundred years, starting in the mid-1800s, the world's largest dolphins—killer whales, or orcas—had humans trained to be their hunting partners in Australia's Twofold Bay near a town called Eden. The killer whales chased large whales into the bay, then actually went and alerted human whalers, who'd come in for the attack. The killer whales understood that they'd get a share of the whalers' kills. The killer whales reportedly even grabbed the ropes attached to harpooned whales to help slow the stricken giants, helping to subdue them.

Spotted hyenas live in societies far more complicated than those of wolves or any other carnivore. Spotted hyena clans have up to ninety members, all of whom recognize one another individually. They understand and use kin and rank relationships when making decisions. Spotted Hyenas also lie. Researchers studying free-living hyenas have sometimes seen this: While higher-ranking hyenas are feasting, a low-ranking hyena falsely calls an alarm that scatters them, then races directly to the carcass for a few fast bites until its clan-mates realize there's no danger. To disrupt hyenas who are fighting with her offspring, a mother sometimes utters a fake alarm-call. A low-status hyena who knows where food's hidden sometimes leads accompanying hyenas astray, later returning alone to claim the prize. Researchers were watching a group that was traveling when a low-ranking male noticed a leopard crouching motionless in a creek bed beside the carcass of a young wildebeest it had killed. None of the other hyenas noticed. The low-ranking male hyena looked directly at the leopard and its kill as he continued past. When all the hyenas were well beyond the creek, the low-ranking male turned and loped straight back, taking the carcass from the leopard and eating—without having to share it with higher-ranking companions.

The problems other animals must solve, and how they must solve them, differ greatly. A human must make a spear; an albatross must fly four thousand miles from her nest to find a meal and then return across thousands of miles of open ocean to an island half a mile wide and find her own chick among thousands. They can't do what we do; we can't do what they do. A dolphin or sperm whale or bat might pity us for staring dumbly into the night when their brains virtually "image" a high-definition sonar world at great speed in darkness, hunting, identifying others, and catching fast-moving food. We might seem as utterly lacking in crucial abilities as they seem to us, disabled by their lack of language—though actually they are extremely enabled in some ways we cannot match. Many creatures blow us away at sight, hearing, smell, response time, diving and flying capacities, sonar abilities, migratory and homing abilities (even under the sea, sensing Earth's magnetic field). Various abilities of many other animals enormously exceed ours. Many are super-hunters. Extreme athletes. (Humans are best at running on two legs—if you exclude ostriches.) Different brains emphasize different abilities, enabling different living beings to excel at different things.

That is reason enough for respectful appreciation, and for a sharing of the world.

CHAPTER 16

Sharing and Caring

Early winter. I've just stepped outside my writing studio. The pooches Chula and Jude are lying in a nice patch of sunlight in a pile of recently fallen leaves. They're not in shade as they'd be in summer. They're doing exactly what we'd do: soaking up the remaining sun, feeling comfy. (Comfort is also why they lie on their pillows at night rather than on the hard floor—except in summer, when the hard floor is cooler.) I crunch a few leaves walking over; they look up at me. Chula is looking me in the eyes, wondering if I come with a request or an offer. I stand still, and her gaze drifts toward the street; the sound of the school bus is familiar to us both. She knows it and has no need to go investigate.

In familiar territory, listening to familiar sounds at frequencies we both hear, soaking up the warmth of this winter sun, we share the same moment. We're using the same senses: sight, smell, touch, temperature, hearing—. I see many colors. They smell many scents, and their hearing is more acute. Our experience isn't the same. But it's similarly vivid. This morning, when I accidently cracked an egg while removing it from our chicken coop, the pupsters were right there lapping it up. We share taste, too.

Shared senses. Why else would they have eyes, ears, noses, sensitive skin, and those adorably sloppy tongues all connected to a brain? Hmm? *Right?—you good girl.* On a winter night, I know how Chula feels beside the woodstove when she's *soo sleeepy* that she can hardly keep her eyes open. Later, when it's time to turn out the light and they're getting onto their beds, I know what that is like because I am doing the same in our shared home, in our shared routine. It's not much of a stretch.

But other aspects of Chula's experiences, of what she senses when we go for walks and she is sniffing, sniffing, and what thoughts and feelings those scents excite—I can't know exactly. But Jude can. Yet I know enthusiasm when I see it, joy when I feel it, love when I share it. There's plenty there.

When Jude, say, chooses between the rug and the sofa, his every action—including his reaction to our coming home and finding him on the couch, where he's usually not allowed—shows his consciousness of choice and the logic of his brain's sensations.

They might not contemplate their own death or imagine next summer's vacation. Neither do I most of the time. In the moment, they're highly perceptive and alert. Except, of course, when they're just snoozing in a sunny pile of leaves.

My dogs are my friends; they're part of my family. I know them better, actually, than I know the people living across the street. I do what I can to care for them and to keep us safe and well. They share more of my life than do my human friends. Like most of my human friends, we're together by accident, and I just enjoy their company. Being around them makes me feel good. Why, exactly? Dog only knows.

Chula often seems to want to know what we'll do next.

Acting hungry, happy, or scared in contexts that make sense to us, so many creatures behave as if they feel humanlike emotions. If you play with a ferret or young squirrel, for instance (or almost any mammal and some birds and even reptiles), you see how much fun they're capable of, and you sense that for some, their play includes elements of humor. On most mornings or evenings, our bottle-reared orphaned squirrel, Velcro, descends from the trees for treats and play sessions. She can easily spend an hour hopping around on our laps and shoulders, wrestling our hands and flipping herself upside down for vigorous belly tickles. We interpret Velcro's vocalizations as a form of squirrelly laughter (she makes *us* laugh, that's certain). Rats playing with one another or being tickled by human researchers produce sounds very much like the laughter of human infants. (Rats' laughing is higher-pitched than humans can hear, but researchers can use a device to downshift the sounds into the human-hearing range.) Rodent fun arouses the same brain area in them that is aroused in human brains by joy. So, do squirrel joy, rat joy, and human joy feel similar? "Young rats we have tickled become remarkably friendly toward us," writes leading researcher Jaak Panksepp. Our squirrel friend, Velcro, can't get enough. We often have to put her back on her big old maple tree and leave her, because we have things like jobs to go and do and can't spend a whole morning just playing. At those moments she seems to have her priorities in better order. She certainly knows how to have a good time. I had no idea squirrels had such interactive playfulness in them, but because we hand-reared her, she revealed a lot.

For full-blown humor, though, apes are the practical jokers. A bonobo (say buh-*no*-bo) is a kind of ape that looks a lot like a chimpanzee. But bonobos have major personality differences; they are much more friendly with one another than chimpanzees. Frans de Waal relates that when the senior male bonobo at the San Diego Zoo descended into the enclosure's dry moat, a junior male named Kalind sometimes quickly pulled up the chain that allowed him to climb back up. De Waal writes: "He would look down...with an open-mouthed play face while slapping the side of the moat. This expression is the equivalent of human laughter: Kalind was making fun of the boss. On several occasions, the only other adult, Loretta, rushed to the scene to rescue her mate by dropping the chain back down, and standing guard until he had gotten out."

All the evidence leads to the conclusion that humans are *not* the *only* conscious, feeling beings who can enjoy living. In other words: life, liberty, and the pursuit of happiness for all. Anyone who plays with a dog—or even a squirrel or rat—sees and interacts with their consciousness.

When a dog brings a ball around to where you're facing, it's because they understand that you can understand what they want. When they're not hungry, they still enjoy a treat.

They *enjoy* a treat.

ACKNOWLEDGMENTS

Any recounting of kindnesses that went into helping me create this book will be incomplete. But let me try: For exceptional help in seeing and understanding wolves in Yellowstone, I benefitted enormously from the singular Rick McIntyre and the amazingly dedicated Laurie Lyman, Doug McLaughlin, and Doug Smith. Their observations, insights, and stories made the wolf sections possible. I also thank Sian Jones for good spotting, Roy O'Connor for introducing me to Rick, and the underfunded U.S. National Park Service for doing its best. Alan Oliver and Mark Miller allowed the use of several of their fine images; I deeply appreciate it.

On the editorial side, my valiant agent Jennifer Weltz has been a skilled and faithful presence throughout. Emily Feinberg and the fine folks at Roaring Brook Press have been wonderful during all this work.

For sharing life, saving horseshoe crabs, closing up the chicken coop at night, and feeding everybody when I'm away (and often when I'm home), I thank my wife, Patricia Paladines, whose love is beyond words.

Not least, of course, I thank Chula, Jude, Cady, Rosebud, Kane, Velcro, Emi, Maddox, Kenzie, Alfie, and so many others, great and little, free-living, domesticated, and in between, who have opened my eyes. From doggies and furry orphans of our living room and yard to the vast seabird colonies of remotest shores; the great fishes, turtles, and whales of deep, wide oceans; the hawks of autumn skies and the warblers of the springtime woods—to those in these pages and all the rest, I offer my delighted gratitude for bringing so much beauty, grace, love, joy, richness, heartache, dirt, mess, and mud into my life. In other words, for making it real.

Thanks, everybody.

Chula and Jude are BFFs!

NOTES

Chapter 2: The Perfect Wolf

9 *Even from a distance:* Smith and Ferguson, *Decade of the Wolf,* 43.

11 *"remarkably gentle":* Ibid., 43.

12 *When packs fight:* Ibid., 72, 87.

Chapter 3: Packing and Unpacking

Wolf pack facts are from: Smith and Ferguson, *Decade of the Wolf,* 88–92.

19 *Extended childcare:* Ibid., 41.

20 *large acclimation pens:* Ibid., 54.

21 *jaws exert twelve hundred pounds:* Ibid., 55.

22 *The Druids traveled:* Ibid., 66.

22 *"tough, supersized behemoths":* Ibid., 68.

23 *Bottlenose dolphins' division of labor:* R. C. Connor in Mann et al. *Cetacean Societies.* Chicago: University of Chicago Press. 212. *See also* Simmonds, M. 2006. "Into the Brains of Whales." *Applied Animal Behaviour Science.* 100 (1–2): 103–16. (Simmonds reviews and cites other sources.)

23 *Humpback bubble net:* Ibid., 211–12.

28 *Wolf matriarchs and wolves Seven, Forty, and Cinderella:* Doug Smith, interview with the author, March 2013, and Smith and Ferguson, *Decade of the Wolf,* 78–79.

Chapter 5: A Shattering of Promises

46 *Lewis and Clark in 1806:* Whittlesey, L., and Schullery. 2011. "How Many

Wolves Were in the Yellowstone Area in the 1870s?" *Yellowstone Science*, no. 19: 23–28.

46 *"Greater Yellowstone Ecosystem":* Goldman, J. G. 2014. "Reintroducing Wolves Is Only Effective at Large Scales." *Conservation,* June 18.

48 *wiped wolves off 95 percent:* Smith and Ferguson, *Decade of the Wolf,* 7–8.

49 *Researchers estimate that 380,000:* Leonard, J. A. et al. 2005. "Legacy Lost: Genetic Variability and Population Size of Extirpated US Grey Wolves." *Molecular Ecology* 14: 9–17.

49 *Over five hundred wolf skins:* Whittlesey and Schullery, "How Many Wolves," 23–28.

49 *No license, no limit:* "Wolves in Wyoming: WGFD Notifies That Gray Wolf Take Is Suspended." 2014. Wyoming Game and Fish Department website.

51 *Wildlife managers pursued eradication and elk populations erupted:* Doug Smith, interview with the author, March 2013.

52 *Aldo Leopold observed:* Leopold, A. 1949. *A Sand County Almanac.* New York: Oxford University Press, 129–32.

53 *Wolves helped liberate aspen:* Ripple, W. J., and R. L. Beschta. 2012. "Trophic Cascades in Yellowstone: The First 15 Years After Wolf Reintroduction." *Biological Conservation* 145 (1): 205–13.

53 *People account for 80 percent:* Doug Smith, interview with the author, March 2013.

54 *"The website Huntwolves.com suggested":* Hull, J. 2013. "Out of Bounds: The Death of 832F, Yellowstone's Most Famous Wolf." *Outside Online,* February 13.

54 *"It's a huge blow"* and *Nathan Varley:* Schweber, N. 2012. "Research Animals Lost in Wolf Hunts Near Yellowstone." *New York Times,* November 28.

54 *"approximately 94,000 visitors":* Duffield, J. W. et al. 2008. "Wolf Recovery in Yellowstone: Park Visitor Attitudes, Expenditures, and Economic Impacts." *Yellowstone Science* 16: 20–25.

Chapter 6: In a Time of Truce

57 *Native American groups have tried:* Pember, M. A. 2012. "Wisconsin Tribes Struggle to Save Their Brothers the Wolves from Sanctioned Hunt." Indian Country Today Media Network, August 14. Online.

58 *"I do not deny":* de Spinoza, B. 1677. *Ethics,* Part 4, Prop. 37, Note 1. Online.

58 *"face-to-face":* Garcia, C. 2010. "'Wolf Man' Doug Smith Studies Yellowstone's Restored Predators." *Christian Science Monitor,* July 20.

58 *Wolves don't view people as potential prey:* Smith and Ferguson, *Decade of the Wolf,* 105.

Chapter 7: Magnificent Outcasts

64 *Old Blue and Fourteen:* Smith and Ferguson, *Decade of the Wolf,* 11.

Chapter 8: Where the Wolf Birds Lead Us

74 *Odin:* Heinrich, B. 1999. *Mind of the Raven.* New York: Ecco, 355.

75 *Ravens' tool kit of reasoning and insight* and *"primate-like intelligence":* Emery, N. J., and N. S. Clayton. 2004. "The Mentality of Crows: Convergent Evolution of Intelligence in Corvids and Apes." *Science* 306: 1903–7.

75 *Raven rapidly solving a puzzle that stumped poodles and toddler: Inside the Animal Mind: The Problem Solvers.* 2014. Video. BBC. (Scene occurs 20 minutes in.)

75 *Crows' intelligence and a crow named Betty:* Emery and Clayton, "Mentality of Crows," 1903–7.

76 *Crow solving an eight-step puzzle:* Packham, C., presenter. 2014."Are Crows the Ultimate Problem Solvers?" Episode 2 of Inside the Animal Mind. BBC Two.

76 *Rook experiments with tubes:* Bird, C. D., and N. J. Emery. 2009. "Insightful Problem Solving and Creative Tool Modification by Captive Non-Tool-Using Rooks." PNAS 106 (25): 10370–75.

76 *Crow shaping wire into a hook:* Klein, J. 2008. "The Intelligence of Crows." TED Talk. Online.

76 *Cockatoos use insight:* Warwicker, M. 2012. "Cockatoo Shows Tool-Making Skills." BBC Nature.

76 *Crows remember faces for years:* Nijhuis, M. 2008. "Friend or Foe? Crows Never Forget a Face, It Seems." *New York Times*, August 25.

77 *"New Caledonian crows and now rooks":* Bird and Emery, "Insightful Problem Solving," 10370–75.

77 *"display similar intelligent behavior":* Emery and Clayton, "Mentality of Crows," 1903–7.

Chapter 9: Wolf Music

80 *Triangle:* McIntyre, R. 2013. "The Story of Triangle." Unpublished manuscript. (McIntyre credits Laurie Lyman with first spotting the wolves that day.)

82 *Music, prosody, pigeon experiments:* Altenmüller, E. et al., *The Evolution of Emotional Communication.* Oxford: Oxford University Press, 116–17.

83 *"Music is one of the best forms":* Ibid., 134.

Chapter 11: A Will to Live

101 *The black wolf grabs the elk:* I thank Laurie Lyman for private correspondence and for her contributions to *Yellowstone Reports* describing some of these incidents.

Chapter 12: Domestic Servants

110 *Wolves can follow pointing:* Udell, M.A.R. et al. 2008. "Wolves Outperform Dogs in Following Human Social Cues." *Animal Behaviour* 76: 1767–73.

111 *"In the midst of the struggle":* Gwynne, S. C. 2011. *Empire of the Summer Moon.* New York: Scribner, 176.

112 *"Get the dax!":* Hare, B., and M. Tomasello. 2005. "Human-like Social Skills in Dogs?" *Trends in Cognitive Sciences* 9: 439–44.

114 *"Humans have had to tame":* Zimmer, C. 2013. "From Fearsome Predator to Man's Best Friend." *New York Times,* May 16.

114 *"Our best friend in the animal kingdom":* Wang, G. et al. 2013. "The Genomics of Selection in Dogs and the Parallel Evolution Between Dogs and Humans." *Nature Communications* 4, article no. 1860. Online.

115 *Darwin on drooping ears and correlation:* Darwin, C. 1859. *On the Origin of Species.* Mentor series. New York: Signet, 34–35.

115 *Russian fox experiment:* Hare and Tomasello, "Human-like Social Skills," 439–44.

117 *Domestication syndrome in foxes and others:* Hare, B. et al. 2012. "The Self-Domestication Hypothesis: Evolution of Bonobo Psychology Is Due to Selection Against Aggression." *Animal Behaviour* 83: 573–85.

Chapter 13: Two Ends of the Same Leash

119 *"An important first step in the evolution":* Hare and Tomasello, "Human-like Social Skills," 439–44.

119 *Changes suggesting that humans self-domesticated:* Quoted in Leach, H. M. 2003."Human Domestication Reconsidered." *Current Anthropology* 44: 349–68.

121 *"had much smaller faces"*: Ibid., 349–68.

121 *Modern versus Neanderthal brain volume:* Roth, G., and U. Dicke. 2005. "Evolution of the Brain and Intelligence." *Trends in Cognitive Science* 9: 250–57.

121 *Summary of Allman's views:* Leach, "Human Domestication," 349–68.

122 *Colin Groves:* Quoted in Leach, "Human Domestication," 349–68.

Chapter 14: Pet Peeves

133 *"Theory of mind" was coined:* Premack, D., and G. Woodruff. "Does the Chimpanzee Have a Theory of Mind?" *Behavioral and Brain Sciences* 1: 515–26.

Chapter 15: They're Not Confused; We're Confused

138 *"When we ask things"*: Thomas, E. M. 2007. *The Old Way.* New York: Picador. 78.

138 *Orangutans evaluate humans:* Cartmill, E. A., and R. W. Byrne. 2007. "Orangutans Modify Their Gestural Signaling According to Their Audience's Comprehension." Current Biology 17: 1345–48.

141 *Dolphins and fishermen in Brazil:* Bearzi and Stanford, *Beautiful Minds,* 230. *See also* Mann et al., *Cetacean Societies*; and Simões-Lopes, C., M. E. Fabian, and J. O. Menegheti. 1998. "Dolphin Interactions with the Mullet Artisanal Fishing on Southern Brazil: A Qualitative and Quantitative Approach." *Revista Brasileira de Zoologia* 15: 709–26; and Daura-Jorge, F. G. et al. 2012. "The Structure of a Bottlenose Dolphin Society Is Coupled to a Unique Foraging Cooperation with Artisanal Fishermen." *Biology Letters* 8: 702–5.

141 *Caroba and Scooby:* Strain, D. 2012. "Clues to an Unusual Alliance Between Dolphins and Fishers." *Science Now,* May 1.

142 *Killer whales were hunting partners:* Mead, T. 2002. *Killers of Eden: The Killer Whales of Twofold Bay.* Oatley, NSW, Australia: Dolphin Books.

142 *Hyenas:* Holekamp, K. E. et al. 2007. "Social Intelligence in the Spotted Hyena (*Crocuta crocuta*)." *Transactions of the Royal Society B: Biological Sciences* 362: 523–38.

Chapter 16: Sharing and Caring

148 *Tickling rats:* Panksepp, J. 2005. "Affective Consciousness: Core Emotional Feelings in Animals and Humans." *Consciousness and Cognition* 14: 30–80.

149 *Frans de Waal and bonobos:* de Waal, F. et al. 2006. *Primates and Philosophers.* Princeton, N.J.: Princeton University Press. 72.

SELECTED BIBLIOGRAPHY

Altenmüller, E., et al. 2013. *The Evolution of Emotional Communication.* Oxford: Oxford University Press.

Beschta, W. J. and R. L. 2012. "Trophic Cascades in Yellowstone: The First 15 Years After Wolf Reintroduction." *Biological Conservation* 145(1): 205-13.

Bird, C. D., and N. J. Emery. 2009. "Insightful Problem Solving and Creative Tool Modification by Captive Non-Tool-Using Rooks." PNAS 106(25): 10370–75.

Caroba and Scooby in Strain, D. 2012. "Clues to an Unusual Alliance Between Dolphins and Fishers." *Science Now,* May 1.

Cartmill, E. A., and R. W. Byrne. 2007. "Orangutans Modify Their Gestural Signaling According to Their Audience's Comprehension." *Current Biology* 17: 1345–48.

Connor, R.C., in Mann et al. 2000. *Cetacean Societies.* Chicago: University of Chicago Press. See also Simmonds, M. P. 2006. "Into the Brains of Whales." *Applied Animal Behaviour Science.* 100(1–2): 103–16.

Darwin, C. 1859. *On the Origin of Species.* Mentor. 34–5.

de Spinoza, B. 1677. *Ethics,* Part 3, Prop. 37, Note 1. Online.

de Waal, F. 2006. *Primates and Philosophers: How Morality Evolved.* New Jersey: Princeton University Press. 72.

Duffield, J.W., et al. 2008. "Wolf Recovery in Yellowstone: Park Visitor Attitudes, Expenditures, and Economic Impacts." *Yellowstone Science* 16: 20–25.

Emery, N. J., and N. S. Clayton. 2004. "The Mentality of Crows: Convergent Evolution of Intelligence in Corvids and Apes." *Science* 306: 1903–7.

Garcia, C. 2010. "'Wolf Man' Doug Smith Studies Yellowstone's Restored Predators." *Christian Science Monitor,* July 20.

Goldman, J.G. 2014. "Reintroducing Wolves is Only Effective at Larger Scales." *Conservation,* June 18.

Gwynne, S. C. 2011. *Empire of the Summer Moon.* New York: Scribner.176.

Hare, B., and M. Tomasello. 2005. "Human-like Social Skills in Dogs?" *Trends in Cognitive Sciences* 9: 439–44.

Hare, B., et al. 2012. "The Self-Domestication Hypothesis: Evolution of Bonobo Psychology Is Due to Selection Against Aggression." *Animal Behaviour* 83: 573–85.

Heinrich, B. 1999. *Mind of the Raven.* New York: Ecco. 355.

Holekamp, K. E., et al. 2007. "Social Intelligence in the Spotted Hyena (Crocuta crocuta)." *Transactions of the Royal Society B— Biological Sciences* 362: 523–38.

Hull, J. 2013. "Out of Bounds: The Death of 832F, Yellowstone's Most Famous Wolf." *Outside Online,* February 13.

Inside the Animal Mind: *The Problem Solvers.* Video. BBC.

Klein, J. 2008. "The Intelligence of Crows." TED Talk. Online.

Leach, H. M. 2003. "Human Domestication Reconsidered." *Current Anthropology* 44: 349–68.

Leonard, J. A., et al. 2005. "Legacy Lost: Genetic Variability and Population Size of Extirpated US Grey Wolves." *Molecular Ecology* 14: 9–17.

Leopold, A. 1949. *A Sand County Almanac.* Oxford: Oxford University Press. 129–132.

McIntyre, R. 2013. "The Story of Triangle." Unpublished manuscript.

Mead, T. 2002. *Killers of Eden: The Killer Whales of Twofold Bay.* Oatley, New South Wales, Australia: Dolphin Books.

Nijhuis, M. 2008. "Friend or Foe? Crows Never Forget a Face, It Seems." *New York Times,* August 25.

Packham, C., presenter. 2014. "Are Crows the Ultimate Problem Solvers?" Episode 2 of *Inside the Animal Mind.* BBC Two.

Panksepp, J. 2005. "Affective Consciousness: Core Emotional Feelings in Animals and Humans." *Consciousness and Cognition* 14: 30–80.

Pember, M.A. 2012. "Wisconsin Tribes Struggle to Save Their Brothers the Wolves from Sanctioned Hunt." Indian Country Today Media Network, August 14. Online.

Premack, D., and G. Woodruff. "Does the Chimpanzee Have a Theory of Mind?" *Behavioral and Brain Sciences* 1: 515–26.

Roth, G., and U. Dicke. 2005. "Evolution of the Brain and Intelligence." *Trends in Cognitive Science* 9: 250–57.

Schweber, N. 2012. "Research Animals Lost in Wolf Hunts Near Yellowstone." *New York Times,* November 28.

Smith, D.W., and Ferguson, G. 2012. *Decade of the Wolf.* Connecticut: Lyons Press.

Smith, D. Interview with the author. March 2013.

Strain, D. 2012. "Clues to an Unusual Alliance Between Dolphins and Fishers." *Science Now,* May 1.

Thomas, E. M. 2007. *The Old Way.* New York: Picador.

Udell, M.A.R., et al. 2008. "Wolves Outperform Dogs in Following Human Social Cues." *Animal Behaviour* 76: 1767–73.

Wang, G., et al. 2013. "The Genomics of Selection in Dogs and the Parallel Evolution Between Dogs and Humans." *Nature Communications* 4, article no. 1860. Online.

Warwicker, M. 2012. Cockatoos Show Tool-Making Skills. BBC Nature.

Whittsley, L., and Schullery, P. 2011. "How Many Wolves were in the Yellowstone Area in the 1870s? *Yellowstone Science,* no. 19:23-28.

"Wolves in Wyoming: WGFD Notifies That Gray Wolf Take Is Suspended."
2014. Wyoming Game and Fish Department website.

Zimmer, C. 2013. "From Fearsome Predator to Man's Best Friend." *New York Times*, May 16.

Dolphins and fishermen in Brazil: Bearzi and Stanford, *Beautiful Minds*, p. 230. See also Mann et al., *Cetacean Societies*; and Simões-Lopes, P. C., M. E. Fabian, and J. O. Menegheti.1998. "Dolphin Interactions with the Mullet Artisanal Fishing on Southern Brazil: A Qualitative and Quantitative Approach." *Revista Brasileira de Zoologia* 15: 709–26; and Daura-Jorge, F. G., et al. 2012. "The Structure of a Bottlenose Dolphin Society Is Coupled to a Unique Foraging Cooperation with Artisanal Fishermen." *Biology Letters* 8: 702–5.

PHOTO CREDITS

INDEX

Page numbers in **bold** indicate illustrations

skills of, 112; orientation toward humans, 1–2, 109–114; playing by, 132–134, **135**, **136**, 141; socialness of, 112–113; swan and ducks encounter with, 129–132; understanding between humans and, 124–126, 149; understanding humans by, 129, 137–141; wolf ancestors of, 2, 3, 107–110, 113–114, 124–125, 128

Dolphins, 23, 74–75, 141–142, 143

Domestication: brain size and, 120, 121; definition of, 107–108; dogs as domesticated wolves, 107–110, 113–114; physical changes related to, 114–118, 120–121; self-domestication, 118, 119, 121–122

Domestication syndrome, 117

Dominance and status, 13–15, 25–31

Druid Pack: Casanova as leader of, 15; character of, 22; Forty as alpha female of, 28–31; litters of Twenty-One and food supply for, 11–12; pup raising by, 29–31; Slough wolves as enemy of, 97; Twenty-One as alpha male of, 10–15, 16, 26, 29

E

Elk: carcasses of, 87; hunting and killing by wolves, 16, 36–38, 42, 52–53, 79, 101, 102–103; hunting strategies against, 24–25; population without wolves to hunt, 10, 51–52; return to Park of, 100; vegetation damage and recovery related to, 51–52, 53; winter territory of, 22, 45–47; wolf injuries from, 21, 24–25

Emi, 133–134